MEDITATIVE MOMENTS OF A SEEKER

ANURAG S PANDEY

Contents

Preface

Neither I am a sage, nor a saint, nor a guru and not even a dedicated seeker. But since my childhood, I have always felt inquisitiveness towards meditation, yoga, spiritual practices, soul and transcendental mysteries. Parallelly I have been in a state of uneasiness to find myself different from others. And despite my sincere efforts, I could not become like them. I had a lot of shortcomings. But they have become my strength now, because I have stopped comparing myself with others. We often forget our path while walking with others. But I am glad that I am on my path towards my goal and simultaneously I am walking with others! This book has some of my experiences related to meditation, which may be useful for you. If those experiences could help you to dive into the depth of meditation, it will be an achievement and a blessing for me. And yes! Not a single line in "Meditative Moments of a Seeker" is imaginary. They are completely visible feelings of a humble seeker.

Introduction

"Meditative Moments" are moments beyond moments. They keep you realizing that you are eternal and infinite. They never leave you from your chase. They keep reviving themselves. They go on getting deeper and more mysterious. They start pulling you. You fail to keep yourself uninfluenced by them. Slowly you drown in them. The doors of the inner world start opening one after the other and you feel as if you are an alien on your planet Earth.

I am in relationship with 'Meditative Moments' since childhood. Sitting for hours in Padmasana (Lotus posture] on the open terrace in the afternoon and playing the game of Meditation. Inviting spirits using planchette and to marvel at their actual arrival, to be effortlessly in continuous state of witnessing. Then came a period of divagation. But those moments walked with me like a shadow and embraced me again.

There is no erudition in this book. If you are interested in experiences related to meditation and you want to delve deeper into those experiences, then this book is for you. It has four chapters.

First chapter is about various experiences of the subtle world. How Krishna, Buddha, Jesus, Sai Baba, Goddess Dhoomavati, Vanadevi (Forest Goddess), Osho, Unknown Monk, Avadhoot Baba Sivananda etc met me in the subtle world and inspired me, helped me.

Second chapter is detailed explanation of various experiences through which a spiritual practitioner undergoes while practicing meditation. For example the feeling of vastness, the pulsation in the penis, the movement of subtle bodies, the spinning and opening of the chakras, feeling the omnipresence of the consciousness, the unfolding of the past and the future, the manifestation of the inner world etc. Why and how do these experiences knock us? Which experiences are positive and which experiences are dangerous to be drowned in? How can we deepen these experiences? I have tried to put light on these factors as per my experience.

Third chapter explains how we can practically use meditation for solving problems. How using meditation we can transform the future, heal physical and mental illness, understand, break and transform thought chains, purify body, mind, intellect and consciousness. And fourth chapter is about the benefits of meditation, how it improves your work skills, helps you set up your goals and so on.

CHAPTER ONE

Experiences of the Subtle World

In childhood dreams I feel I am 40 years old

I was four or five years old when I had that dream first time. Second time I was seven years old and I was nine years old when I had that dream for third and last time. No one could decode that dream to me. Was that my previous birth? Why I had the same dream again and again? These questions were constantly chasing me.

The view was visible from inside the train. The train was speedily leaving behind open fields and grasslands on both sides. After a few moments the scene changed. There was a fort with water around. The scene changed again. I was inside the fort. I was climbing up the stairs built on the fort wall. But I was not like me. Yet I was feeling that this is me. I was forty years old! I was in cream colored kurta-pajama (Shirt & Trousers). My body was muscular and height was medium. My face was slightly round. I had long mustaches and dark complexion. I climbed up the stairs and came on the terrace. A thirty years old woman was standing there. She was in Rajasthani or Haryanvi dress. She met me and treated me lovingly. Then only an old man came from behind. Maybe he was my father or uncle. But for sure he was a family member. Also he was in kurta-pajama. His hair and mustache were white. He looked at me with a smiling face. I was feeling happy and familiar with them. But suddenly their expressions changed. A cruel, frightening, distorted and disgusting expression appeared on their faces. I felt deceived. They were playing a deceptive game with me. I was alarmed but it was too late. Before I could save myself, they had pushed me down from the terrace of the fort. They had planned to make me a prey to crocodiles.

I abruptly came out of the dream here and remained sleepless. Did they kill me? Could I save myself? What happened next? Was it me?

Childhood experience of flying in sitting posture

I was 6 years old. I knew nothing about meditation. I used to go to the yoga center in my locality to learn yoga. One day I was on the cot at home. Mother was folding clothes nearby. The cot was next to the window. The window was open and the farms were visible. There was a road beside the farm. A row of trees was dividing them. There were iron bars in the window. Purposelessly I sat in Padmasana (lotus posture) and closed my eyes. I had learnt this posture in the Yoga Center. As soon as I closed my eyes, I saw myself flying out of the window in the same state, in the same sitting posture with eyes closed. My body went out of the window, passed over the farms and started flying amidst the trees. The window bars were no more obstacles. I freely passed through the window bars. Being bewildered I opened my eyes. I saw that I was sitting on the cot! Later I understood that it was my subtle body which flied through the window. This was one of the experiences during deep meditation.

To feel divinity, purity and cleanliness all around after the school prayer

Perhaps this is everyone's experience. I was in third or fourth class. After mass prayer in school, when I opened my eyes, I could feel the difference in the surrounding. Everything was looking fresh, clean and divine as we feel after taking a shower. Later I realized that this too was a spiritual experience. When we witness the self with pure consciousness, everything outside appears in its natural form that is divine. We begin to experience divinity in everything. When we close our eyes, we come closer to ourselves and when we open our eyes, the state of witnessing remains active for a while.

The Tantrik worshipper of Mother Kali who sent help through his obedient good spirit

I was soon to step into the nineteen springs of my life. For some time a spirit was troubling me. Though, I was not taking it too seriously. I had a belief that I could protect myself by meditating whenever I would want. First of all, I should know about that soul. I should know that why that soul was interacting with me? But in fact I was falling into that spirit's trap gradually. That soul was playing with my emotions. There was a small temple of Goddess Kali near our house, in which a sadhak priest lived. He was an exorcist. He looked like an Aghori. His left eye was damaged; eyelid and skin around the eye had become black and thick. He used to pour out the scent of any flower from his hand. Sometimes he used to produce the fragrance of the desired flower from the hand of visitors. I thought that I should share my problem with him. May be he could help me. When I told him about the troubles being given by a soul; he chanted some mantra and saw something in his palm. Then he again chanted some mantra and blew on my face and said that now no soul will be able to trouble you.

That night, as soon as I went on the bed and closed my eyes, I could clearly see a divine person was standing by my head in an alert posture. He was dressed like ancient warrior. He had a spear in his hand. His expressions were furious. His eyes were burning like embers. With those burning eyes he was unblinkingly looking at my whole body. I felt that he was protecting me. And I saw that the soul was not able to touch me. The presence of that warrior was not allowing the soul to come near me. The soul appeared to be disturbed. And then the soul started befooling me emotionally. Unfortunately, I got caught in the maze of emotions and sent that soul a mental invitation. As soon as I invited the soul, the warrior sent by the priest of the Kali temple disappeared. And that soul again entered me. However, I got rid of that soul much later; after learning a lot of lessons.

But on that day I learnt how important our wishes are! That warrior had to return only to honor my wish. Nature also respects our wishes. Also God grants boons according to the wishes of the devotee. That is the reason sometimes even a boon becomes a curse. So, we should be very careful about our wishes.

The sympathy from a stray dog helped me overcome a suicidal move

In Tatanagar there is a Pahari Maa (Hill Mother) temple on top of a hill which is famous as "Golpahari". There are several hundred steps to reach the temple. There is a sharp downhill at other side of the hill. I was twenty years old. Defeated by the circumstances, I decided to end my life by jumping from the Golpahari hill. It was about to get dusk. Consolidating my intention, I was climbing up the steps one by one. From the very first step, a dog had started climbing with me. The dog was climbing up and climbing down but not going three or four steps far from me. I did not pay more attention to the dog. I thought it was asking for food. I had built a stone wall around my feelings. So I did not feel sympathy for the dog. I reached the top in some time. On the other side there were sharp rocks hundreds of feet below. If I jumped, I was sure to die. Before I would jump, I sat on the bench for two minutes. I was fast recollecting my whole life for the last time. Now any moment I was about to get up and jump down. Then only the dog came and hugged my feet and started crying too badly. I realized that this was not normal. Dogs come and ask for food or lick our feet, wag their tail. But this dog was crying too badly. The dog was rubbing its body on my feet. At that very moment I understood that the dog was crying and sharing my sorrow. I was going to commit suicide. There was some great misery inside me, which I had closed with a very hard cover. The dog could feel the pain and perhaps knew what I was going to do. So, the dog shared my grief. The stone wall around my feelings melted because of the dog's unusual gesture. I loved that dog for a while. I felt lightheaded and I gave up that suicidal attitude.

Feeling of self pervasion throughout the city

It was a different kind of experience. I was with a friend. We were walking on the road while talking to each other. Suddenly I felt my physical existence getting expanded all over the city. For a moment it felt as if my body has become very large and pervaded the whole city. A few days ago I had given some of my poems and pictures etc. in a newspaper for publishing. The very next day after this experience, that newspaper published some of my poems with my picture. It definitely increased my popularity and the people of my city came to know about me. It means that fame or popularity is related to the subtle world and events take place first in subtle world and then they take place in the physical world.

First experience of distant healing through meditation

I was a tutor of two brother and sister in a family. Brother was in class eighth and sister was in class ten. Once the sister did not attend the class for about 15 days. Being queried, their mother told me that she was ill. She was not recovering despite taking medicine. That night when I was meditating, suddenly a thought about that girl appeared in my mind. I developed a feeling of compassion for her. She became live in my mind. She was on her bed. She was looking sick. I could see circle or slightly oval circle around my body. The circle was transparent. Its periphery was made of blue light. I realized that I am capable. I can do whatever I want. I sent a thought wave to that girl – "Child, get well!" And I saw light beams twice coming out of my head and going to that girl. It was a healing process for just a second or two. Or perhaps it was just an inspiration or motivation. The next day I was surprised when the girl attended the class and she was perfectly fine. Seeing her, I realized that she had experienced something last night about which she could not say anything. Perhaps she must have seen me in her dream or she must have heard my thoughts.

Experiences related to Balayogi Shri Sadananda

The hilly area of Tungareshwar Mountain starts at a distance of seven kilometers from Vasai Road railway station in Palghar district of Maharashtra. The famous Tungareshwar Temple of Lord Shiva is four kilometers inside the hilly forest of Tungareshwar. Tungareshwar hilltop is seven kilometers from the Temple. Monastery of Balayogi (one who becomes a sanyasi/monk in early childhood) Shri Sadanand was situated there. Someone had told me about that monastery. But I did not know how far it was from the temple. Once I visited Tungareshwar temple alone for darshan. After I offered prayers to God Shiva, I asked the priest about the monastery of Baba Sadanand. The priest told that Baba Sadanand's monastery is just nearby. Yet I asked him that how far the monastery is from there? He replied that it is only a short distance away. I decided to meet baba Sadanand and I hiked up the mountain road to reach his monastery. It was a winding unpaved road. It was afternoon and I was walking on that winding road alone. Till temple passersby could be seen often. But after the temple it was very rare to see a passerby because very few people visit the monastery in the hilly forest area. So I found myself alone. On every turn I was finding another turn at the end. I thought that there would be Monastery on the next turn. But there was turn and turn only after the other. The priest had said that the monastery was just a short distance away. Had he told that the monastery was seven kilometers away, I was sure to return from the temple only. Maybe that's why he lied to me that the monastery was only a short distance away. After walking for a long time, I saw a bike rider coming from front. I asked him how far the monastery is. And he replied that it is 3-4 kilometers far from there. What could I do now? So I decided that when I have come so far, I will definitely go to the monastery of Baba Sadanand.

After a few turns, a funny incident welcomed me. At some distance a troop of about 15 small and big monkeys was standing in a line on the path. They all were staring at me. The last monkey in the queue was their leader, who was standing ahead of all by keeping his right hand on his waist. I did not understand what to do now? Should I fight these monkeys or go back? I thought I did not have any violent feelings for them. Then they too should not attack me. I kept on going a bit hesitantly. As soon as I started getting very close to them, they all ran and climbed up a tree a little inside the unpaved road. I laughed at their behavior. They again stood in a line on the path little further and were staring at me. This time I felt it funny as I was moving forward. As soon as I got closer to them, they again ran and climbed up the tree. It was a game for them. Were they really playing with me? Those monkeys did not come back after repeating this 4-5 times. I kept on moving forward.

In those days it was unsafe in Tungareshwar forest due to leopards. Also it was heard that a tiger lived in that forest. But I was going towards the hilltop fearlessly. I was not worried that it would be late evening while returning and the forest would become more dangerous in the dark. On the winding road of that deserted hill, there was a deep valley on one side and a sharp hill on the other. Then suddenly I heard tiger's growling from the depths of the valley. This was the first time when I had heard such a growling outside the sanctuary. For a moment I halted. I estimated that if the tiger sensed my presence, it would take him less than a minute to come up. The monastery was still about two kilometers far from there. Then at some distance in the path side bushes, I heard unknown wild animals attacking each other. I had no option but to escape. There were unknown wild animals ahead and a growling tiger down the valley. I closed my eyes to make a decision. I saw a huge meditative form of Sadanand Baba on the huge rocky wall of the mountain in front of me. I took it as his blessing. I opened my eyes and started moving forward. Now I was not afraid of anything.

In some time I reached the place of Baba Sadanand. There I had some free drink made of herbs, sipping which all my tiredness disappeared. There was a temple of Baba Sadanand's Guru Baba Nityananda. After bowing my head in the temple, I tried to meet Baba Sadanand and came to know that he had gone to the other side of the hill to examine the herbs in the forest. In the hope to meet him, I was climbing down at the other side of the hill. Also it was an unpaved path. After walking for a while, I saw Baba Sadanand. He was accompanied by a young disciple and an elderly lady. The woman had a gentle expression on her face. I called out 'Babaji'. Baba turned. He looked about forty years old. There was a permanent smile, peace and divinity on his face. I quickly moved to touch his feet. But he stopped me with a gentle gesture. He used to talk very little. I could not stop myself. Then only his disciple sternly asked me to stop saying that no one is allowed to touch Babaji. But I wanted to touch his feet. So I went ahead. Then only I felt my feet staggering. And something like a spark hit my toes. I stopped immediately. I looked at Babaji. Still there was a gentle smile on his face. Babaji raised his hand and blessed me. Now the disciple had a gentle expression on his face as well. I stood watching them. Babaji left in the jeep with the woman and the disciple. I stood there for a few moments feeling the divine presence of Babaji. Then I returned feeling blessed.

For several days after that day, when I sat down to meditate, Babaji appeared to inspire me to go deeper into meditation. He was still blessing me in my meditation.

Goddess of Tungareshwar forest appeared before me

After a few days I again visited Tungareshwar temple with some friends. Then we went to Baba Sadanand's monastery also. It was afternoon. We were having fun while walking on the path through the mountain. The surrounding nature was very beautiful. Suddenly at one place I started to feel very different. A different kind of happiness, peace and divinity spread around there. In my inner mind, I saw a small flying human shadow a little down in the valley side walls. I did not tell anyone about this.

We reached the monastery. It was dusk while returning. Due to the fear of wild animals no one was ready to return except me. Everyone decided to spend the night in the monastery itself. I accepted the decision of majority. The staff of the monastery told us that they will arrange free food for us. They asked us to reach the dining place at

8 o'clock. After roaming around a little bit, we came to the dining place at exactly 8 o'clock and sat in the line with others. We were hungry and eagerly waiting for the food. Some people from the monastery were also sitting with us. After sometime the organic plates made of leaves were placed in front of us. The thought relaxed us that the food will be served now. But food was not served. And all of them started singing psalms. We were morally forced to sing psalms with them. It was really a fun. We were laughing and hunger was killing us. After about half an hour of singing, food was served. The food was very simple. The food had rice, pulses and some wild vegetables, which we ate for the first time. The food was luscious and satisfying. Then we went to sleep in the hospice built in the monastery. We were given a big common hall to sleep. The floor of the hall was covered with a carpet. There were no additional beds available except that carpet. We were given blankets. There was a huge picture of Baba Nityananda on one side wall. We decided to keep our head in that direction only. We used to sleep usually after twelve o'clock in the night. But there at 9 o'clock we were feeling sleepy. I was feeling a mysterious calmness in the hall, as blessing was being poured there. At 4 o'clock in the morning, I woke up on my own. I was surprised because I used to wake up after 7 o' clock. We realized the profound effect of the environment on us. We returned to our homes.

A few days later, one night, I was at my friend's house. I was sitting in Padmasana (lotus posture) and practicing meditation. After a long time, suddenly I began to see the same place of Tungareshwar Mountain again and again where I had felt some divine vibrations and had seen a mysterious flying tiny shadow. After a few moments with closed eyes I saw a young woman's hand (palm, fingers) in a blessing posture appeared before me. The hand was divine. I had never seen such a beautiful hand. And then the shape of the whole body began to appear. A very beautiful young woman, dressed like a goddess was appearing before me. I thought that she is definitely a goddess and at the same time the thought of her being a woman also came in my mind. And then that figure appeared in the form of Ardhanarishvara (lord Shiva in form of half man and half woman in one body). My hands automatically joined with obeisance. I began to feel a strong scent emanating from my hands. Tears started rolling down from my closed eyes. I felt my every pore was melting. After a few moments the figure of Ardhanarishvara disappeared. I wept for a long time and kept thanking the goddess for appearing before me. I also thought that the goddess wanted to appear before me in form of goddess only. But since I had thought of her being a woman, that is why she took the form of Ardhanarishvara. Mother! I offer my prayers to you! Appear before me again, mother! And this time appear in form of goddess only, mother... In those days a soul was residing in my testicles. To move the soul out, I covered my testicles with my palms which had the holy fragrance of the goddess. I felt that the soul was in agony as soon as I did this. The soul could not stand the holy energy of the goddess. After hitting the walls of the testicles several times, the soul somehow came out of the testicles in the form of an energy explosion. The soul had left my body.

Sudden experience of my own subtle body

In those days I used to go to the Brahma Kumari's center. They play very influencing, helpful music during meditation session, listening which it becomes easy to enter into deep meditation. I was meditating while sitting in Sukhasan (relaxed posture). Both my hands were kept on my thighs. My palms were open in the upward direction. I was trying to get into the depths of meditation with the help of music. Suddenly I felt my right hand rapidly moving up and down. And then also my left hand moved like that. Both my hands were moving up and down randomly. I opened my eyes and saw that both my hands were motionless. As soon as I closed my eyes, I again saw both my hands moving rapidly up and down. I understood that these were not my physical hands but my subtle hands. I continued meditating. And then all of a sudden I felt myself going out floating through the window of second floor apartment. Then floating I landed down on the street and walked on the street. Simultaneously I was meditating in Brahmakumari's Center and walking on the street. I understood that later was my subtle body. During sleeping I experienced my subtle body many times. While sleeping, I wanted to turn sideways. But I was not taking turn. Suddenly my subtle body took a turn in the desired direction. My physical body was still in its previous state, while the subtle body was laid on its desired side. I felt both the bodies simultaneously. And now I had no requirement of taking turn. It means subtle body is superior to the physical body.

Visualizing a scene from thousands of miles away with eyes closed

After engagement I was desperately waiting to get married. I was missing my fiancé. She was 1800 km away from me in her hometown. I laid down and closed my eyes and started thinking about her. Suddenly I saw circular waves coming out from inside my head. And then an oval screen appeared in my mind, in which I could see the real time telecast of my fiancé. My mother-in-law was sitting in front of door. My fiancé was massaging oil on her hair by standing behind her and then sitting on the chair. Then she combed her hair. After a few moments the scene disappeared. I called my fiancée and asked her, what she was doing just the moment before? She told me the same thing what I had just seen. When I told her about this, she could not believe me. I told her about style and color of their clothing. She was surprised. For me this was an experience of unplanned telepathy. After this, I practiced telepathy several times, in which I was successful many times.

I underwent a similar experience while I was talking to a female friend on phone. I had never met her. While talking, a desire to see her appeared in my mind. And after a little mental effort, I started watching her live in my mind. She was talking to me while laying on left side of the bed in a room with her stomach downward. Her face, complexion, clothing, color and design of bed sheet, furniture of the room, paintings on the walls, decoration and everything was clearly visible. I started telling her all the details. She was amazed as I was telling her the exact details. She laughed and joked that it was good that she had not called me half an hour ago because then she was in a towel. I laughed and said, 'I might not be able to see her then, because the subtle mind knows better what to see and what not to see.' I was struck and amazed by these mysterious abilities of the mind.

Creating imaginary scene in friend's mind by sending mental waves

In those days I was practicing and testing abilities of mind. Deciding a number in mind and through mental waves asking a friend to think that number only. And then verbally asking the friend to think any number in mind. Then telling the friend that he or she has thought that number only. Almost every time that friend had thought the same number. Or else verbally asking the friend to secretly choose any finger of any hand in mind. Then I try to visualize the unknown chosen finger. I visualized all fingers in my mind and think that the chosen finger will shine amidst all fingers. Then I try to visualize that which finger is shining. I happen to see two-three fingers shining. Then I came to a conclusion that which finger is shining actually. Finally I tell the friend that he or she has chosen that finger. Almost every time I correctly found the secretly chosen finger. Then once I thought to do a deep experiment. I was in the office with a friend. We had some free time. I asked him let's play a game. I will try to transmit imaginary visuals in your mind silently using mental waves. You will keep your eyes closed and will try to receive the imaginary visuals transmitted by me. Let's see what happens. He got ready for this experiment. We closed our eyes. I started imagining natural visuals and transmitting the same to his mind. Beautiful morning, snowy mountains, huge lake, white lotus blooming in the lake... After that I opened my eyes and asked my friend to disconnect the telepathy. The friend as soon as opened his eyes yelled out that what a beautiful scene you showed me sir! You made me joyful! The snowy mountains, the lake, the white lotus blooming in the lake... Now I was surprised to hear this because I did not expect success to such an extent.

Experiences related to Asaram Bapu

Every day we hear news about corrupt Babas (saints, monks, guru). Asaram Bapu is one of them, who is sentenced in jail. I do not know how true or how wrong is he. My mother says that when these baba does hard work for attaining mystical powers, they receive those powers. They receive God's blessings. Using those powers they influence millions of devotees and acquire immense wealth. And then Maya (worldly illusion) dominates many of them and they go in the path of sin. I have experienced some truth in this. In those days Asaram Bapu was a stain free popular spiritual Guru. He had billions of followers all over India. People used to read his magazines. People worshiped him. I was not a devotee of any Baba. I used to meditate and read literature related to it. Then there came a slight disorientation in my life. Instead of meditating, my mind started wandering on other things. Then one day while meditating, I saw Asaram Bapu. He looked at me angrily. He shook his body wrathfully, as if jerking me to come out of the disorientation. I had no emotional attachment with him. Yet he came to my psychic world and inspired me. From this it is clear that he used to travel in the subtle world. This shows he had spiritual powers. But later he might have strayed from the path of spirituality.

Experiences related to Osho

I used to read Osho's books passionately. I practiced his guided meditations too. I felt connected with him. In those days I was too much worried about my chakras. All my chakras were blocked. I felt like I was imprisoned inside my body. No fly, no leap, no excitement was accessible. I could not even lift my consciousness above my head. As if someone had tightened a small round iron skillet by placing it upside down on my head. Or as if my head was covered with poured molten iron. One such night when I tried a lot to meditate, I completely broke down and I called out in my heart, “Osho! Look at my condition! You say that anyone can dive into meditation in any circumstances. I am not able for so long! What should I do?" Suddenly I saw shining Osho in a glowing robe in the deepest darkness around. He was in tall dark blue robe and diamond studded cap. The sky was black all around. Osho looked at me and without saying anything he raised his right hand, pointing upward with his index finger. I followed his finger. The sky was completely black everywhere. Full of darkness. And when his finger went up and stopped, I saw that there was something like a sun in the middle of the sky, which was shining with divine light. And after a few moments Osho and his surrounding disappeared. I realized that Osho wanted to tell me that there is only one solution to my problem that I have to travel from darkness to light.

Sai Baba of Shirdi appeared and blessed me

Many people consider Sai Baba of Shirdi as God. In my vision he is saint, a miraculous man. I was unmarried at that time. I along with my family had visited Shirdi Sai Baba’s Temple. There suddenly a monk came to me and said, "You will be fine." I could not understand why did he say this to me? Did he know about my problem? I did not pay much attention to him. We returned back to Mumbai our home.

We reached late at night. I sat on the sofa. I casually looked at big painting of Sai Baba which was hanged on the front wall. Sai Baba was standing next to a hut with his right hand raised in blessing posture. A cow was standing nearby. The painting had some trees, grass, huts and village scenery. As usual, I had looked at that picture. And suddenly that picture got alive. Sai Baba, the leaves of the trees, the cow, everything got alive. There was a wonderful radiance and brightness in the picture. Rays of light came out from middle of Sai Baba's right hand palm and started entering me. I was just thoughtless on seeing Sai Baba alive in front of me in the painting. Before I could understand anything, everything was back to normal. Painting was again as simple as before. But I knew something wonderful had happened. There was no deep devotion in my heart. Still Sai Baba showered his grace on me. He appeared before me. May be because I had a pure heart.

Miraculous Powers of Baba Imtiaz Hussain Ashrafi of Dungarpur

Babaji of Dungarpur used to visit Mumbai once in a month. Thousands of people met him in his camp looking for solutions to their problems. Babaji cured physical, mental, spiritual disorders using Mantra, mysterious healing power and herbs. He used to remove stones just by keeping hand on stomach. He also neutralized Tantra-Mantra, black magic etc. At that time I was going through a strange problem. I felt as if some external force had made its home within me. I was unable to remove that energy from my body. When I meditated, I felt as if a 4 inches tall person climbed up from the lower part of my spine, holding my spine like a pillar. One night, I sat in Padmasana posture (Lotus Posture) and with strong determination I began to meditate deeply. After about an hour, as usual, I started experiencing severe pain in my legs and joint bones at hips. Somehow, I kept on tolerating the severe pain which was increasing every moment. After some time I felt some restless energy inside my body in lower back. That energy was colliding on my body walls. And the pain I was suffering moments ago had gone. I continued to meditate. And then that external energy came out of my testicles with a strong jerk. He was a 4 inches tall man. He jumped down from my thigh, walked fast and entered under the sofa kept a few feet away. I felt that I had won and I got up. But while sleeping, suddenly that energy again entered my body and resided there. So finally I went to Babaji's camp and I told him that perhaps I am suffering from some black magic. Babaji checked my pulse. I saw a concerned expression emerging on his ever smiling face. Babaji told me that I would have to go to his residence i.e. Dungarpur. There he will be able to solve my problem.

After few days I went to Dungarpur, Babaji's house. He lived there with his family. In a hall a chair table was kept next to a wall. Babaji was sitting on the chair. He was meeting people one by one and solving their problems. There was a small cell in the wall at a height of three feet, where a big lamp was burning. It was dark inside the closet. That area was looking like a cave. The hall was crowded with troubled people. I was waiting for my number. Babaji was solving people's problems by reciting mantras and waving hands. When my turn came, Babaji asked me to bow my head on the platform of the closet. I followed his command. Babaji asked me for a handkerchief and by holding it in his right hand he started rolling it on my stomach. I did not know what he was doing. After some time he got success. He pulled out something from my stomach and showed it to me. I saw a small figurine covered by the handkerchief. It was about four inches long and three inches wide. The figurine was of a young fat monster with bald head. His mouth was wide opened and he had pulled out his long red tongue. He was wearing rings in his ears and was wrapped some leather around his waist. By his outfit he was looking like a tantric or demon from hundreds of years ago. I asked Babaji what is this you pulled out from my stomach? Babaji laughed and said that this is that black magic. Now you should return. I will keep it imprisoned at my place. Saying this, Babaji threw that figurine in the dark cave like closet. I returned from there. But that figurine monster had somehow freed itself from there and had reached my house in Mumbai within an hour. When I spoke to the elder sister on the phone, she told me that she had seen the same type of evil man entering the house. But his height was normal.

Even after that my problem was not solved. I met Babaji again. And he helped me to come out from the clutches of that devil.

Spiritual help received from BK sisters

In those days I used to spend one hour daily in Brahma Kumari's Center for several months. The sisters there were very cordial. They are very spiritual and affectionate. Many of them have the ability to read your mind. I started visiting their center to know about their knowledge and Raja Yoga method. On the very first day while sleeping at night, Brahma Baba came in my dream. He was just looking at me. The next day while I was waiting to fall asleep, suddenly I felt as if Brahma Kumari's sisters were sitting around me and they were all consciously looking at my whole body. Then I started feeling pricking of needles in my chakras. I got scared for a moment - "Are these Brahma Kumaris doing some black magic on me?" But after a few moments I came out of this illusion. Because the soul, which was living in my body, had just tried to enter my body. But as the soul touched my body, it received a strong shock and moved back sharply. I understood that BK sisters were behind this miracle. They were healing my Chakras. They helped me.

After this, almost every night when I practiced meditation by sitting in padmasana (lotus posture), after about one and half hour, a bunch of thousands of light dots traveled to me from distant sky and entered my room through the closed door and stayed near me for some time and then went away. After a few days I understood that they were in fact BK Brothers and Sisters and other meditation practitioners from all over the world. While meditating they merged their consciousness into light dots and met together and travelled the world. They noticed my meditation waves and got attracted towards me. So they came to me. May be they wanted me too to join their company. This happened for several days.

In BK Centers BK sister or brother first read Murli (daily spiritual message from Brahma Baba). Then they explain the meaning. Then they help the visitors to practice Rajyoga or say one kind of Meditation. During meditation they work hard on subtle level to help the visitors to have deep experience and grow spiritually. One day during the meditation session BK Sister looked at me. I saw two swirling rings of blue light appeared in her eyes and travelled directly to me and entered my eyes. I trembled a bit. Once during meditation session, BK Sister's subtle body came to me flying in her sitting posture. She made a hold on my left upper arm and uplifted my astral body in the air. Once BK Sister in form of astral body jumped from her meditation seat, crossed more than 10 feet and reached me. And waving her right hand she cut my astral body into two parts from top to bottom which became again one in less than a second. Once a BK Brother while giving me Prasad (food after offering the God), had a divine look at my forehead for a few seconds. In this way they awaken the soul and the third eye chakra. He stared at my third eye chakra for a few moments. The next day when I woke up, I saw a light shining inside my third eye. I understood that BK Brother's divine look had a good effect on me.

They do special programs on Mahashivratri. For that event BK Sister had asked me to write some poetry. One afternoon when I started thinking about the poetry, I entered into a deep meditative state. I started feeling my body huge like a mountain. I wrote a four-line poem for their event, which one BK Brother recorded in his voice for the event – "Deep darkness got spread. Every person has become alone. Maya spread its dreams on everyone's body and mind..." These were those lines. At the end of their another event, when they played the meditation music, after some time suddenly I started feeling the fragrance around me and I saw that Brahma Baba (subtle body) had come there and was going to everyone and blessings them by extending his right hand towards their forehead. He came to me too and blessed me. The scent had intensified that moment. When the music stopped, I opened my wet eyelids and I saw the BK Sister standing far in a corner. She was already looking at me. I felt as if she had seen Brahma Baba blessing me. BK Sister looked happy for this. It was a relationship of spiritual affection.

Buddha showered waves of light on me

Once I had visited Bodhgaya. There I sat on a bench near the Bodhi tree and started meditating with my eyes closed. Suddenly I saw that a bunch of hundreds of gentle light dots appeared little above the Bodhi tree and rained down on me. I opened my eyes in astonishment. I was overwhelmed. I looked at the tree. A foreigner lady was sitting on a bench nearby. She was looking at me. I looked at her and understood that she had seen dots of light raining down on me. Well... I started thinking why did Buddha bless me? Would that day ever come in my life when I would be able to attain self-realization? And Buddha could have showered grace on me without even expressing it. Then why did he express? Is he prompting me to meditate deeply...? Maybe this was the truth.

Jesus poured his fragrance upon me

Years ago I watched the movie "Passion of Jesus Christ". The pain he had tolerated for the truth; was absorbed in my innermost self. If he wanted, he could have avoided his suffering. But he did not do so. My heart was filled with reverence for him. A few days later I was walking with a friend. A church was on the way. We just went inside the Church and came out after offering prayer. A small statue of Jesus kept in a glass box was placed on the Church's wall outside. Seeing the statue of Jesus, I again remembered "Passion of Jesus Christ". I stood under the idol and bowed my head in reverence with folded hands and praised the Jesus. And at that very moment I felt as if the statue of Jesus was spraying fragrance on me. The fragrance rained on me for a moment or two. I understood that my feelings have reached Jesus. And he too has showered his love on me. I began to think that if the messengers of God are so great, who exist beyond the limits of time and space, then how great would be the God. Then this thought also came to my mind that why did Jesus show his grace to me? Was he prompting me to enter the spiritual world?

Danced with Gop-Gopikas and Radha Krishna?

After the engagement, I, my fiancee and some members of both the families together went to visit Jagannath Dham Puri temple. It was my first visit to Puri Jagannath ji temple. Despite too much crowd we worshipped lord Jagannath comfortably and returned back. I and some of my family members were staying at my fiancée's house. When I was waiting to fall asleep in the night, suddenly I started to feel an unknown fear. Some strange energy was being felt around. After a few moments I started seeing many trees and monkeys in my mind. I thought that after a long time, I had spent a lot of time amid the temples, trees and the monkeys; that is why I am seeing all them now. The feeling of fear was over by this time. Then suddenly a curtain opened inside my head. The opening of the curtain was in a circular form, rotating in a circle. And I started receiving divine visuals. The scene was probably from ancient time. There were trees all around. There was an open space in the middle where men and women were dancing in a grand manner. Everyone's clothes were old fashioned. Men were in dhoti, colorful round kurta and turban. Women were in Ghagra-Choli (long skirt-Blouse) and ornaments. Everyone had garlands in neck, etc. I was also one of them, a man. Dressed and decorated like them. My face was different too.

There was a platform under a tree in front. The pair of the most divine woman and man was on that platform. Also they were dancing. We were dancing in joy and ecstasy. The couple on the platform looked most divine. And it seemed to me as if that couple was the source of our joy. After a few moments the visuals disappeared. I opened my eyes. I have not even slept yet. I was still waiting to fall asleep and I saw it like a dream. I thought they were Radha, Krishna and Gopa Gopikas. And also I was a Gopi. And we all were dancing in the maharas (divine dance of Radha Krishna with Gop Gopikas). Then I thought that maybe it was some previous birth of mine, in which we were doing Raas (divine dance) in the memory of Radha and Krishna. Whatever it was, but there was some relation of Krishna ji or Puri Dham with me. Perhaps Jagannath ji showed me this dream only to remind me of the same relationship or else the memory of my previous birth had been emerged after coming to Puri Dham after births. There was definitely some secret behind this dream which I had watched in waken state.

Experiencing ghastly and then gentle form of Goddess Dhoomavati

To meditate on goddess Dhoomavati, I had a meditation music, in which there were chants, mantras and so on. This music was for an hour intense meditation. This was my first time meditation on goddess Dhoomavati. It was evening. I switched off the lights of the room and lit a lamp. While meditating I saw with my closed eyes that a middle-aged woman came and sat next to me. Her appearance and presence were very gentle and loving. I was feeling good in her company. Despite her extra long nose I had no weird feeling. For a long time the woman sat next to me. Then she left. After the completion of meditation, I told my family members about that lady. They all started saying that goddess Dhoomavati had come to you. Her nose is very long. I had not seen the picture of goddess Dhoomavati till that time. Later, when I saw the picture of goddess Dhoomavati, I was filled with pleasant, exciting surprise, because the same woman had come and sat next to me, while I was meditating on goddess Dhoomavati.

The next day in the evening I again did the meditation on goddess Dhoomavati. That day suddenly Dhoomavati mother came to me in her formidable form. I found myself in space in front of the formidable goddess. I was sitting. Mother was standing. She started eating my head. I surrendered myself without fear. She kept biting my head with her long teeth. Then the visual disappeared. Later I realized that goddess Dhoomavati was devouring my demerits and impurities. And since she had to come in her formidable form and she did not want me to be scared of her, that's why she had come to me on the first day in her gentle form. Wake up, wake up, goddess Dhoomavati mother, wake up, wake up Dhoomavati mother, I pray you mother... I would like to say one thing here that when you meditate on any deity for the first time or you worship a deity for the first time, that deity definitely blesses you with divine experiences despite your little effort. That deity makes you to feel his or her presence. That deity makes you to remember your relationship with him or her. But after that such experiences do not happen again and again. After that you have to do intense meditation and spiritual practices continuously. Then only they help you. It is same like this; in the pre nursery, the teachers have a lot of fun with the children. But then year after year the amount of fun is reduced a bit and the amount of seriousness is increased a bit.

Sudden appearance of a delicate cloud above my head while meditating in the room

In those days I used to chant Gayatri Mantra. I had not taken initiation from a Guru. One day in the morning, I was chanting the mantra by sitting in Vajrasana (a sitting posture). About half an hour later, I suddenly saw a bright delicate cloud high in the sky. It speedily came down and reached above my head in the room. The cloud was whitish. It was spread over a radius of five to six feet. It had reached right above my head and was probably about to enter my head. Then I got scared. As soon as I was afraid, the cloud disappeared. I opened my eyes. I felt that I had deprived myself of some important achievement. I do not know what it was? Was that divine knowledge or divine blessings? Was it cosmic energy? Was it divine grace? Was that a spiritual accomplishment? I do not know what that thing was. But undoubtedly it was related to the spiritual world itself.

Unknown monk saved my life

Due to depression, I had decided to commit suicide. It was late evening. I took in eighty blood pressure and sleeping pills and started wandering on the roads. After a while the pills started showing its effect. I was seeing everything burning, emitting smoke all around. Time factor was disappearing again and again. Each time the duration of disappearance was increasing but the gap between the occurrences gradually reduced. Then I returned home carefully. I was trying my best to have control on myself.

I did not want anyone to know about my condition. So I carefully went to my bed. I was one hundred per cent sure to die in a few moments. A thin thread of life was going to break any moment. When I closed my eyes, I saw my existence drowning in the infinite ocean of darkness. All I could say in mind was - "Death hug me!" And at that very moment some miraculous waves swirled inside my head and I began to see a visual.

It was about to get dusk. Forest, small river, 4 monks crossing the river. All this was visible from across the river. It indicated I was on this side of the river. But I had no body. In fact I was absent yet I was visualizing. The four monks crossed the river while walking. Then the youngest monk, who was in back of three monks stopped, turned and smiled. It was as if he had given smile to me.

I do not know what happened after that. I woke up at normal time in the morning. I felt refreshed more than usual. The pills had no effect on me. I was surprised. And I remembered the monks who had appeared at night and the youngest monk who had given me a smile. I felt as if that monk had saved my life last night. Who was that unknown monk? I wanted to know this. Even today I do not know him. But he definitely knows me, I feel so.

Spiritual experiences related to Avdhoot Baba Dr. Shivanand

Till that time I had not taken initiation from any guru. My elder sister had attended Shivyogi Avadhoot Baba Shivanand ji's Shiv yoga camp a few days back. From there sister had brought some meditation music CDs recorded in Babaji's voice. I used to practice meditation in different ways. So I played Babaji's music CD and started meditating.

After some time, suddenly I began to see a very influential middle aged seeker in ocher cloth wrapped around his waist and kept on shoulder. His huge body, his wheatish complexion, his big and heavy face, his sparkling eyes, his huge hands, big palms and so on. He was worshipping a goddess. He was putting sacred Kumkum on goddess' forehead with his palm. He was chanting Mantras. His half closed eyes were lifting upwards. I was shocked that who is this seeker? I opened my eyes and told my sister about this. Sister said that Babaji looks like this. Sister showed me Babaji's picture. I was stunned because I was seeing this person only while meditating. I wondered why Babaji had appeared before me like this.

After a few months Babaji was to come for initiating seekers for Durga Saptashati Beej Mantra sadhna. At the behest of my sister, I got myself registered for this spiritual learning camp. When I saw Babaji on stage in the camp, I was seeing him for the second time. For the first time I had seen him while meditating. There was a crowd of thousands. As soon as Babaji started the dialogue, I understood that Babaji was able to simultaneously read the thoughts of each and every person present there. He was selecting his dialogues according to thoughts of seekers. Some of his words were a response to my thoughts. I was overwhelmed to see this extraordinary spiritual ability of Babaji. It was as if he already knew me and as if he had already thought that he would initiate me for spiritual learning. There were many divine experiences during Babaji's spiritual learning camp. I felt my subtle body. I experienced my higher self who was not a young man like me, but a child aged eight or ten years and who was smarter than me. In a deep meditative state, I saw people with whom I felt I had a deep connection, but whom I did not know in this life. After completing the spiritual learning session in that camp, Babaji told all of us that from now onwards one of his forms will live with every seeker individually. He has gifted everyone a form of himself. That form will be with the seekers every moment and will help the seekers in their spiritual journey. If the seeker would commit any mistake, his form will explain to the seeker not to commit the mistake again. But even after repeated explanation, if the seeker continues to make that mistake, then his form will leave the seeker and come back to him and get absorbed in him. I started thinking how is this possible? How can one Babaji be with thousands of seekers every moment! Babaji had read this thought of mine. He laughed and started saying that Shiv Yoga is science beyond science. Nothing is impossible in Shiva Yoga. A shivyogi (seeker of lord Shiva) can read mind of millions peoples simultaneously. I thought to examine the truth in his words. Anyway, the three days camp was over now.

When I returned home that day, I did not feel anything that would make it seem that Babaji's form was with me. I thought that Babaji had not said that seriously. By the way, I had already seen the miraculous powers of Babaji. I just could not understand how it is possible to take thousands of forms at once. That night when I laid on the bed to sleep, I saw clearly in my mind that Babaji appeared from nowhere and laid peacefully next to me. I was watching him in my mind laid beside me. He was as calm as if he was in a meditative state. The energy of his calmness started to flow towards me. My mind became completely calm. My thoughts stopped completely. I started sleeping in the depth of meditation. The negative energy that often troubled me was not visible around. And then it became a daily routine. Throughout the day, Babaji did not appear near me at all. But as soon as I lay down to sleep at night, he used to appear calmly next to me. I understood that Babaji knew that I had problems while sleeping. That's why he stays with me during my sleeping time to save me from those problems. And one night I took beer before going to sleep. I was slightly intoxicated. I thought that now I have become impure. So today Babaji will not come to me at all. But as soon as I laid on the bed to sleep, Babaji's form appeared and laid down next to me with the same calmness. I was stunned. It means Babaji had seen the purity of my heart and not the impure beer in my body. I felt guilty that because of me Babaji's form had to sleep next to the person who had taken beer. Babaji's form remained with me for many days. But then one day Babaji's form left me because I was constantly ignoring his gestures and getting entangled in negative thoughts. Later I felt very sorry because I lost something very precious. I pushed my spiritual growth prospects too far back. After that, even after trying a lot, Babaji's form did not come back to me. Alas, he could live longer with me. But I had sent him away from me. Two things I liked most about Babaji's form; first his presence created calmness and second he seriously took care of others self respect. He calmly indicated the mistakes of seeker. But he never forced the seeker. Keeping respect of the wish of the seeker, he used to keep silent.

After a few months, Shivanand Babaji's son Ishaan Shivanandji was initiating the seekers for Pratiprasav Sadhana (Method for spiritual rebirth). I attended his spiritual session. Like his father, Ishaan was able to read everyone's thoughts in a crowd of thousands. He was a little younger than me, which I was thinking again and again. Then how can I take divine knowledge from him? Replying my thought wave Ishaan ji told the seekers (indirectly to me) that even though I am younger than most of you in age, you can take divine knowledge from me because I have the ability to give you the divine knowledge. It is not the age of the Guru, but the capacity of the Guru which counts. After that, during the spiritual camp, he first took the seekers into a state of deep emotion. Then by saying emotionally reasoned things, he tried to take the seekers into the depth of samadhi or meditation. Thought came to my mind that what he was saying, could have been said in a better way. That would have created a deeper emotion. And then I was taken aback when I heard Ishaan ji saying the same thing. I was thinking what Ishaanji should say. And then Ishaanji was saying the same words after few moments. He was not doing this because my words were needed. He could even move the seekers into a state of deep meditation with his words. But he chose my words because he probably wanted to show me the extent to which talent can be carved! To what extent can you go beyond your limits! Perhaps he was prompting me to plunge into the infinite depths of meditation.

During the same spiritual camp I realized that Shivanand Babaji had also come there invisibly and there were many other high level seekers who were invisible and who were secretly helping the seekers to get into meditation. During the same spiritual camp I saw two black moles formed on my index finger and palm. So fortune is changed during spiritual practice. I experienced this. My wife had thyroid disease, due to which she was not conceiving despite medical treatment. She was undergoing treatment for the last two years. But till now there was no benefit. Ishaan ji told that Babaji (Shivanand Babaji) had come (Though I knew this because I had seen him.) and has blessed everyone. Within ten days everyone will definitely get some good result. Everyone will definitely get rid of one or the other problems. And then in the crowd of thousands as if Ishaan ji looked directly into my eyes and said, "Babaji has performed a miracle on someone at this very moment. You have been blessed with boon of child." I started thinking that would the pregnancy report come positive this time? And this was exactly happened. Only a few days later, her urine pregnancy test showed a positive result. And after 9 months we became parents of a lovely girl baby.

Once I had gone to Babaji's meditation camp with my family. Babaji was in another hall. We were watching him on the big wall of the hall using projector. A grumpy person was sitting next to me. He said about himself that he has done this sadhana, he has done that sadhana (spiritual practice). Then he asked me, which sadhana have you done? With the intention of shutting his mouth, I started telling lies that I have done this sadhana and that sadhana, the sadhana which he had not done. At that very moment Babaji's soft laughter was heard on the speakers. I immediately understood that Babaji had heard our conversation which had made him laugh.

Once I went to Babaji's monastery. Babaji was not there. He had gone to some other city for teaching Shiv Yoga (the spiritual method to emerge infinite within) to seekers. There was a crowd of seekers in his monastery. There was arrangement for everyone to meditate and receive Prasad (meal) etc. I meditated with everyone. Then I took the prasad. While returning, I felt as if Babaji was standing in the corridor on the first floor and watching the guest seekers. His body was slightly bigger than his actual body. His expressions were like that of the host while sending off the guests. Babaji was present there even though he was physically absent. And he took care that every person who came to his place should get respectful hospitality. But did other seekers also see him standing in the corridor? Perhaps not every seeker saw him but certainly some of them. Some advanced seekers must have also talked to him. But why did I see Babaji? Maybe he was telling me that he is always connected with seekers. Or perhaps he was encouraging me to move faster on the spiritual path.

When Babaji teaches Shiv Yoga to seekers, in between the teaching he sings bhajans (religious song). As soon as he starts singing bhajans, he pushes the seekers into the depths of meditation. The seeker starts feeling like a small child. Babaji says “Sabkuch Bhava Re” (“emotion is everything”). Then how can meditation go beyond "feeling"? Yes, in the deepest state of Bhava (feeling) it may be that we find ourselves at that highest peak of feeling, where the kingdom of feeling spreads just below. While meditating, I myself have realized that when I remember the Guru or God passionately before meditating, I quickly reach at the state of deep meditation. So Babaji helps a lot while meditating. When seeker calls him, he comes. He helps, guides and makes the spiritual path easier for seekers. Especially when you are in trouble and you remember Guru or God with a sincere heart (if you are in trouble, you will remember Guru or God with a sincere heart only) then he helps immediately and makes you to feel his presence directly. Babaji has got me out of trouble every time! But sometimes Guru brings difficulties in your life so that you could become strong and overcome your weaknesses. Babaji has made me experience this too and my heart will always be grateful and indebted to him for this.

CHAPTER TWO

Experiences during meditative moments

Meditation is not an action that you can start doing it. Meditation is to watch the action taking place and to watch the doer doing it. But watching is also an action, is it not? The act of watching and watching the doer is meditation. It is moving from subtle to more subtle. It must have been difficult to see the image of self when there was no mirror, right? Even today, living beings who do not use mirrors, how would they see themselves? What category would they put themselves in, the beautiful or the ugly? I think absence of mirror has curbed their disorientation. If all the mirrors are destroyed, then our disorientation will also stop to a great extent. I am not just talking about the glass mirror. We are in the habit of using our own minds and the minds of others as mirrors to understand the real and fake images of ourselves. Due to this we forget our true nature. As such we forget what we could be, what we could attain, how far we could have blossomed and what could be our destination. We destroy all those possibilities. Re-creating these possibilities is meditation. To feel the true false veils on oneself is meditation. Watching your unconsciousness consciously is meditation. This meditation can be done by sitting, walking, even working. One can be in meditative state even while sleeping. We wake up every morning from sleep. When we wake up from our unconsciousness, then that is meditation. When meditation happens, when we fall into meditation or when meditation rained on us, then we undergo many experiences. Different states of meditation have different experiences. Some of these experiences are the creation of our imaginations, while some reveal the secrets of the inner world. If you practice meditation, you must have had similar experiences. You may find it useful to read these experiences. There may be no increase in your knowledge after reading them. But it will certainly inspire you to fly into the inner sky, to dive into the depths of meditation.

Experiencing vastness

In the state of meditation, it is felt many times as if your body has become many times bigger. As if you are spread across the room and your head has reached close to the ceiling. You begin to experience vastness sometimes in your whole body and sometimes in some of your body parts. Sometimes you feel that your palms have become hundred times bigger. Sometimes you feel that your head has become very big. Sometimes you feel that your body has become bigger than your home. And sometimes you feel yourself huge like a giant mountain. Along With vastness there is another experience you undergo during meditation, that is to feel lightness. Big body but light body, weightless body. Besides this you start feeling a vacuum or an ether or celestial element within your body. When you undergo these experiences, at the same time, you start feeling that you are powerful and capable of doing anything. You feel like you've become impenetrable. You feel as if you are able to materialize anything just by your will. As if there is no inferiority left in you and you do not even need anything anymore. As if you are complete. I have these kinds of experiences often. But this experience does not remain constant for long. These experiences usually last for about fifteen minutes. But sometimes even for half an hour I have remained in this state. During this time you get rid of all kinds of negative energies and thoughts. You get healed at a deeper level. Your mind becomes calm. You start experiencing someone in you is witnessing. You start feeling grateful to the creator. Your faith in God increases. And if you are an atheist then your faith in your atheism increases too. You become more original. During this, you become free from both the past and the future and you start living in the present moment.

When you practice meditation regularly, you automatically start feeling the vastness. You start feeling vastness all of a sudden. You feel vastness when your consciousness transcends your physical body and enters the subtle bodies. Sometimes you feel vastness even when you are not meditating. You are completely immersed in some work. And suddenly a fountain of unexplained bliss bursts within you. You are working and you do not know that who is creating this joy within you. Along with this joy, you may feel vastness too. If you feel the same while working, then also that is an experience of meditation. Meditation is not just sitting without doing anything. Meditation is a deep awareness towards external and internal events. Meditation is a rhythm between bodies, thoughts and consciousness. To watch this awareness and to feel this rhythm is meditation, which can happen either while sitting or working. I loved writing computer programs. Sometimes writing a program on the computer continued from night to morning. During that time I have sometimes experienced what I experience during meditation. I experienced vastness and unexplained joy.

Experience of changing body direction virtually during meditation

I have had this experience many times. By sitting in Padmasana (Lotus posture) or Sukhasana (relaxed sitting posture) I was trying to dive into deep state of meditation with my eyes closed. Then all of a sudden I started feeling my body turning diagonally in the right direction. When I opened my eyes, I saw that my body was sitting in the same previous direction. I closed my eyes again. After a moment, again I began to feel my body sitting diagonally in the right direction. I had this experience many times. Sometimes I felt my body turning its' direction in right side and sometimes on left side at more or less degrees. I do not know the actual reason behind this. But I think it can be related to the direction of the magnetic energy currents of the earth or it can also be related to cosmic energy. As we know, the earth has south and north magnetic poles. Earth's magnetic waves keep flowing in a particular direction, which has an effect on our body and mind. That is why there is a scientifically approved belief in India that one should not sleep by keeping head towards north direction. So it may be that while meditating, my subtle body used to adjust itself in the most appropriate direction. If it is so, then surely the direction has an effect on meditation. There is some direction which is best suited for meditation. And this direction can be different on different parts of the earth.

Sweating armpits

While meditating, when sitting in any posture, sometimes suddenly one or both of your armpits start sweating. Is it so? I often experience this. When my armpits sweat, I understand that in a short time I am going to go deeper into meditation. And it really happens. It is good if your armpits sweat while meditating. This is probably due to the production of some hormones in the body. While meditating, many chemicals start forming and transforming in our body. This makes it easier for us to go through many spiritual experiences. The feeling of joy is also due to the production of some hormones. Sweating from the armpits while meditating brings a special kind of purification as if the body has expelled the impurity in the form of sweat. And now the body is ready to go into deep state of meditation.

Feeling cold, warm air or energy flowing towards the body

You must have had such experiences. There is no change in the surrounding environment. Even then suddenly you feel touch of a little hotter or a little colder very calm air or energy at some of your body part. And then gradually that heat or that coldness starts spreading throughout the whole body. Mostly it starts from the upper part of the head. Sometimes there is a feeling of warmth or coldness in the whole body as if some external energy is entering the body. Sometimes you feel the same thing in your spine from bottom to top or from top to bottom.

In my experience, the feeling of coldness while meditating is auspicious. It is divine grace or blessings from well wishers who have already progressed on the spiritual path. It helps you to grow spiritually. But the experience of warmth is not auspicious always. However, when someone sends you healing, you feel warmth. You feel warmth when other/s use their energy to push you deep into meditation. But sometimes it can be negative energy too. A spirit or some Tantra applied on you. Therefore, when experiencing heat, one should be little alert. At that time it should check whether this heat energy is helping you to get deeper into meditation or is distracting you from meditation. You should not welcome this heat energy if it is distracting you.

Feeling of sparse or condensed energy waves moving around the body

When I was new to this experience, for several days I could not understand what was happening with me. I was trying to immerse myself in deep meditation by sitting in a posture. After a long time passed, I started feeling an energy flowing on the outer edge of my body. This energy was in the lower part of my body, which was slowly moving round right to left, front to back. Gradually the energy started condensing and also its speed increased. But due to severe pain in the hips joint bones, I could not sit for long and got up. Then it did not happen for several days. Then after a few days, I had this experience again after sitting in meditation for a long time. This time the energy was denser than before. It was covering lower two to three chakras of the body. After this many such experiences happened. Then one day came when this energy started moving around my whole body like a whirlwind, at a stormy speed.

It was moving around my whole body, in all the chakras. I felt as if my body was in the middle of a tornado or a cyclone. After that I started getting deeper into meditation. My thoughts began to stabilize dramatically. I started to witness thoughtlessness or gap between thoughts. Slowly I understood that while meditating, the experience of energy waves circling the body is auspicious. It is a sign that your consciousness is transcending the physical body and is taking you to your astral level. It is taking you beyond body, beyond thoughts, beyond mind...

Everything in this universe is made of energy. Energy is hidden within what we see. Our body, intellect and mind are also made of energy. Meditation is a way to transcend all your boundaries. While transcending, energy also moves from one level to another. That's why we undergo these kinds of experiences.

Experiencing divine Aroma

Once I went to a temple with a friend. The friend was ahead of me. As usual a railing was fixed on the door of the idol room, so that the devotee could not go inside the room. So we stood at the railing and looked at the idol with folded hands. Then my friend bowed his head on the railing with devotion and started praying. As he bowed his head, I felt a scent coming to him. Some part of that fragrance was coming to me too. But that fragrance had come for that friend only. I understood that it was God's grace in the form of fragrance and I had also received a little part of it.

Like form and colour, smell is also a medium of expression. Or it may be that the smell tells the reality of that object. We can deceive anyone with our manipulated looks and colours. But can we do anything with the smell that is being emitted from our existence? We can cover ourselves with perfumes. But we cannot hide our real smell. A person who has control over his or her senses, will easily catch our real smell and will know our reality. Our food habits, our thoughts and emotions affect our smell. Through meditation we can improve our smell. You must have heard the elders saying that the evil spirit is foul-smelling and the fragrance spreads with the arrival of a good soul. Similarly, deities, angels and great spirits also spread divine fragrance. There are many types of fragrance which can be due to different proportions of different virtues. The fragrance or bad smell that we emit reflects the level of our consciousness. The higher our consciousness rises, the better our smell becomes. We offer flowers in temples, mosques etc. because flowers do have fragrance and this is a divine quality.

When we are absorbed in meditation, sometimes we feel different types of fragrances being emitted from our body or around our body. This happens because of two reasons. First reason is that our consciousness starts rising up due to which good energies and spirits get attracted towards us or come to us or shower their grace on us. And second reason is that meditation purifies body, mind and soul. Due to this our thoughts are created at higher level and our consciousness expands. This produces fragrance within us or our smell starts transforming into fragrance. So whatever would be the reason, it is an auspicious sign to feel aroma during meditation. Whether little or big, but meditation definitely brings change in the quality of your smell. You can check it yourself. Before you start meditation, smell your palms carefully. And after meditation, smell your palms again. Did you notice any change in both smells, little or big? You can also do another experiment. Sit down and think negative. Keep thinking. Start thinking negatively so deep that you would forget that you are acting. After a while you would find that your existence is producing a foul smell. If you could feel the bad smell, you would never think negatively. How can you allow anything in your mind, which smells bad?

Experiencing electric waves forming circles and producing sparks

You must have heard that the human body is the most complicated machine. This is actually a fact. But is the structure of an atom not complex? The existence of such small particles like electrons, protons, neutrons moving on their orbits with balanced speed and are in bond with each other with balanced power of attraction and repulsion. Is it less complicated that particles or atoms are performing their job without error? Does God exist or not? Was this universe created by someone or it was created by itself! Whatever be the truth! But no one can deny that the Universe is extremely complex and systematic. For the creation of the universe or the existence, the consciousness, the supreme consciousness were either created or they were already present? Then birth of energy took place. Space, direction and time were originated. Then the very fine particles were created or they were formed on their own. And it is not confirmed that these tiny particles are electrons, protons and neutrons. The search for still smaller particles is continuing. Then the space was expanded. The five basic elements were created. The sense powers were created. Planetary constellations were formed. Then a time came when the earth came in existence and an environment suitable for life to flourish on it was developed on it. Rivers and oceans were formed in a natural process. The water cycle took birth. Just as the veins carry blood everywhere in our body, similarly rivers carry water to every corner of the earth. Where there are no rivers, there are springs and ponds. Also rains fulfill this task. This system not only supplies the water but it also purifies the water, recycles it for reuse. The life cycle came to existence. Millions forms of life were created. All living beings dependent on each other for survival and food. Such a system was auto created where creatures by eating each other help the life cycle to exist. If there were no tree then cows, deer, etc. would have starved to death. If there were no cows, deer etc., then the carnivorous would have died. If there were no cows, deer lions, etc., the trees would have died because who will convert their oxygen into carbon dioxide! Well we come back to the point that human machine is the most complex machine which is more complex than super computers. Then also our capabilities should be better than supercomputers. We should be better than supercomputers in memory storage, recalling ability, speed, accuracy, calculation etc. Also we should be better than TV and Internet in sound and visual communication. We should be expert in telepathy. Unfortunately almost all of us are ignorant of these capabilities. We are so complex that we can become devils or we can become God if we wish. You must have seen machines. They contain complex circuits. Electric or magnetic energy flows in them. Energy is converted in the parts of the machine. Machines communicate with each other through invisible waves. Satellites give us data. We should also have similar capabilities. In fact thousands of times more sophisticated capabilities than that. Electricity and other waves also flow inside us. Our thinking is also a kind of wave which can go anywhere in the universe. We just have to learn to control it.

While practicing meditation our dormant energies begin to awaken. Due to which the movement of waves in our body increases. We start creating new types of waves. We begin to receive external waves. During this, we sometimes experience telepathy. Electromagnetic waves start flowing rapidly in our body. Sometimes they become more condensed or they dissipate due to obstruction in their transformation, then we feel them, like formation of a round blue circle of electric waves around the body. In that state, hitting the nail on the ground produces a small round blue whitish flame with the sound like 'chattt'. Or Feeling like a short circuit while removing any physical or mental impurities.

But mostly this experience is auspicious. This is a sign that your energy is getting integrated. You are getting ready to leap into the higher and deeper dimensions of existence. With a little practice in this state, you can experience telepathy. But there is no need to stress much on telepathy because telepathy is your innate ability which you are just unaware of. Your goal is to know your capabilities and to go beyond them, beyond all your abilities...

Experiencing flood light

To experience light is a spiritual experience. Each chakra present in our body emits light of different color. In normal condition, these chakras and the color emanating from them are not visible. But in the state of meditation or yoga, they become visible. If chakras radiate blackish color, it's sign of impure energy or impure chakras. That is why bad energy is called black or dark energy. Unsatisfied souls appear as black smoke. Similarly, as much our energy and our chakras get purified, their true colors begin to bloom. When fully developed, all the colors merge into white light.

When we practice meditation, our consciousness begins to rise and we begin to enter deeper into the existence. Then we start seeing our chakras and so on. We begin to see our energy body and light waves of different colors. We start seeing white light flame between the eyebrows. Its colour keeps changing. A slightly different colour effect is visible little above the head. Some shiny light dots start appearing. Sometimes all the dots appear integrated. Apart from this, light waves coming from the outer sky are also visible. Like a ball of light or a cloud of light or a ring of light starts coming towards us, enters inside us and gets lost. In fact nothing in this universe is disconnected with each other. Everything is connected to each other. The whole existence is intertwined, visibly or invisibly. That is why it is said that there is God in every particle. Every single particle is connected with God. (Atheists can replace God with something else in their own way here.) We are connected to the whole existence. So there must have been an exchange of energy and other things between us and existence, right? Something will emerge out of us and merge into existence and something will come out of existence and merge into us. We see the exchange of five elements. But we are not able to see the exchange taking place at the micro level. In the state of meditation, we start seeing that subtle hidden exchange. We start seeing light coming out from within ourselves and merging into the universe and light coming from the universe and merging into ourselves. It is not that this exchange of light takes place only while meditating. Rather, this exchange is happening every moment. While meditating we are able to see it. Though it is also true that the quality of the energies that we exchange with the universe increases while meditating. We begin to make a positive impact on the universe. So in return the universe also starts showering its grace on us. It is auspicious to see light waves or beams of light while meditating. This is a sign that we are getting deeper into meditation and our spiritual growth is taking place.

Experiencing pulsation in the penis

If you are a woman, you can understand the vagina instead of the penis. When I started practicing meditation, after a few days I started feeling like a pulsation in the penis while meditating. The penis was getting up a little again and again. You must have noticed that the penis of a small child moves up while the child is sleeping. Sometimes this happens even when the child is awakened. I was experiencing something similar. There was no increase in size of penis. There was no sex feeling in my mind. Still the penis was pulsating again and again and there was a feeling of joy due to this happening. I thought that I am not even thinking about sex then why is my penis pulsating. Is something going wrong? Will I ejaculate? But nothing like that happened. I understood that this is not related to ejaculation. After that I started experiencing this more often and realized that it was my fundamental energy that was being awakened. My energy was trying to rise. Shakti (Feminine energy) was preparing to meet Shiva (Supreme Lord). The union between nature and man was forming. It was an experience of self-intercourse too. Every woman is a combination of half woman and half man. Also every man is half man and half woman. Men and women fall in bondage of attachment and love for each other only to find their other incomplete part.

The tree is the development of the seed. Life is born from a seed and becomes a tree. Seeds have reproductive power. Similarly, the reproductive power works in the penis and vagina and linked organs. Life energy is most deeply attached to it. The smallest and biggest changes in life pass through the same center of energy. This center of energy cannot be bypassed. You cannot develop directly to your upper chakras. You have to develop from the first step itself, that is, from your Root chakra, which is near your penis. When your energy flows down from the penis you can have children and if your energy starts flowing upwards from the penis you can create your soul. Though, the soul is eternal, immortal. But in your personal experience the soul will not exist until you help your soul to take birth. The vibration of the Penis is the beginning of that journey which starts from the Root Chakra and reaches up to the Crown Chakra and continues towards the infinite. Pulsation in the Penis is due to the awakening of the Root chakra and rising of the energy. One should not think wrong on having such an experience and should not let your mind to wander elsewhere. Just keep watching your rising energy with a witnessing attitude. It's a very auspicious experience. There is a feeling of great pleasure in this. And there is spiritual growth too.

Feeling of the anal area contracting upwards

While meditating you may experience this also. Suddenly you start contracting your anal area upwards again and again. In this, you also use the muscles on both sides of the lower end of the spine and the muscles of the hips. You are trying to pull something up. It is an experience connected with the Root Chakra. The energy which was flowing down from Root Chakra now wants to rise. Therefore, to push it upwards and to close the downward way, the anal area thus starts to contract upwards. When this happens, pleasant waves start rising upwards in the body, mainly through spine, and reaches up to head top. You begin to feel tickling or sensation. For more pleasure we begin to try to pull the energy up by contracting the anal area upwards. If you do not do this then you should. While meditating, if you feel that your anal area is contracting upwards, then you should cooperate with this and help your energy rising upwards.

Experiencing the waves rising

This too is the experience of rising energy. You are sitting in meditation and suddenly energy waves start rising in your body. Energy starts rising in your spine, as well as it rises from the right and left sides of the spine. As they rise up, they reach the back of your head and both the sides. The energy waves then condense into the circular region in the upper part of the head. These waves give a feeling of happiness. It also makes you to feel tickling, inner trembling, sensation etc. It's a great experience. This is a sign that your energy wants to rise and you are about to go deeper into meditation.

Feeling of joy and ecstasy

While meditating, suddenly, without any reason, mind starts feeling joy and ecstasy. The mind starts melting. It feels as if the body is also melting. It becomes clear that I am not the mind of “I” or the body of “I”. The "I" begins to merge into the Infinite Existence and the Infinite Existence gets merged into the "I". Sometimes I feel that I am not only within myself but also within all human beings. Not only within human beings but I am present within all animals and insects too. And not only within animals and insects, but I am present also within trees, grass, rivers and everything. Then it seems as if there is no existence of "I". On intervals thoughts occur and go away. You are watching them. Sometimes imagination takes you far away to the unknown. You come back again and again. You seem lost in a game. You start creating different type of wonderful worlds. Your imagination becomes so strong that you become bewildered and mesmerized by your own creation. Sometimes you reach the moon and sometimes you embrace the sun. Sometimes you start roaming in a forest near a waterfall or river, or sometimes you start tying bonds between you and your favorite Goddess or God or you create a symbol according to your ideology and create a unique relationship with that. You would say that this is a fantasy. So there’s nothing wrong in that. This imagination is good because it is creating good energy around you. Gradually imagination will subside and the real infinite will be unfolding around you more and more. Imagine a couple who are going to get married very soon. Do they not envision the days they would spend together after marriage? Similarly, when we meditate, our goal is self-realization. But the problem is that we are not acquainted with the soul or the Supreme Soul. So we start using imagination. It is reasonable.

And fantasy and reality depends on your state of mind. For the common man the world is reality and the dream is a fantasy. But for a yogi, even the world is a dream.

And it may be that this world is actually just a figment of some divine power. Imagination is a power that can create the world from nothingness. You can create your world with the power of your imagination. And in fact you do create. You have made a person a bad person. You have made a person a good person. And what is bad for you is good for someone else and what is good for you is bad for someone else. So this is a wonderful harmony between fantasy and reality, is it not so? So sometimes because of our imagination and sometimes due to the grace of God, we start feeling joy and ecstasy while meditating. And this feeling also happens because while meditating we start returning to our center. Bliss is always naturally present in our center. So it is natural to feel joy and ecstasy while meditating. But drowning in it is not your goal. Let it happen. Stay focused on the target.

Feeling extreme pain of separation

Sometimes, while meditating, you suddenly start experiencing intense separation. You and your every pore start crying and burning to meet the unknown whom you do not even know. These are really tough moments. You must have experienced pain of separation for your boyfriend or girlfriend in your life. Our love with God is infinite times deeper than that love. For an atheist, this love can be with nature. Still, you simply remember that God lightly like anything. In fact you are separated from God. When you get separated from your boyfriend or girlfriend, you start to suffer. This separation is so painful for you. But even after being separated from God, with whom your love is infinitely deeper, you live very comfortably. You are not burnt to ashes in separation. Do you know why? Because

Maya has put a veil between that love and you. Sometimes while meditating, a hole is done in the veil of Maya and you begin to feel your love for God. At that time you feel intense pain of separation. You and your every pore begin yearning to become one with God. You find your whole existence put on fire. You forget the whole world. You become crazy in the love of God. However, in some time Maya manages to repair that puncture in the veil and you come back. What if you failed to come back? If Maya fails to repair that hole, then you are bound to wander madly in the love of God. And nothing could be better than this! Well, experiencing intense pain of separation while meditating is very painful but a very auspicious experience. The more painful you feel this separation, the more peace your soul receives. This experience is a sign that your grip of Maya is weakening and you are getting closer to the Divine element.

Crying and laughing without reason

Once I was doing active meditation. I was jumping on my toes. After that in that part of meditation, when you leave your body calm, suddenly I started weeping without any reason. I was seeing myself crying bitterly. I could see that I was calm but someone in me was crying badly. And the interesting thing is that he too does not know any reason for that grief. I did not stop it. I kept crying for some time. And then suddenly my act of weeping stopped itself. And at that very moment a fountain of laughter erupted in me. Now I was surprised to see myself laughing. I was weeping a moment ago. And now I was laughing like an insane. That too for no reason. I witnessed myself laughing. I was not laughing. Somebody in me was laughing. I was experiencing this. After a few moments, the act of laughing stopped suddenly. I found myself standing in a state of absolute peace. I witnessed someone in me weeping with heart-wrenching pain and then laughing with exuberance of joy. And I witnessed someone in me completely untouched in both these states. I witnessed someone who was untouched by sorrow and happiness. I thought what had happened to me. I realized that grief and happiness are stored within us. We keep accumulating them gradually. Grief wants to come out but we suppress it inside. We hide the grief. Joy wants to make us crazy. But we hide it. So both the emotions keep accumulating. Similarly, also other types of emotions are stored. And sometimes on the slightest thing, any of these emotions floods out like a dam breaking. This is what had happened that day while meditating. Meditation purifies. It purified my mind. It released stored grief and joy. This experience also makes it clear that the soul, or consciousness, is beyond both pleasure and pain. If you experience this, you should welcome it.

Redness of eyes and conscious mild intoxication after intense meditation

Once in an insignificant road accident my wife and my daughter got some injuries. At night I started healing them by chanting Mahamrityunjaya Mantra. I was chanting the mantra very passionately and I continued this for a long time. I kept praying to Shiva. The more I was getting immersed in emotion, the more I was getting Shiva's and Guru's grace. After some time I felt a slight conscious madness inside me. I started talking with Shiva. Then after some time I chanted the mantra. Then again I was talking with Shiva. For hours I sat in the same way sending healing. After that for two days I noticed, my eyes were red and

I was feeling little intoxicated. Without consuming any intoxicant or cannabis etc. And those who came in contact with me, they too felt that I was little intoxicated. They started asking me that have you taken any drug. Have you eaten cannabis? But this intoxication was not such that one could not control himself. I had complete control over myself. But a slight intoxication, a slight euphoria, a little carelessness, a little joyful, I was feeling in my behaviour. I remember, earlier also people used to tell me that looking at your eyes it seems that you are a drug addict. I told them that I do not take drugs. But they never believed it. Even then I used to meditate. Maybe even then I was little intoxicated due to meditation, which I could not understand that time.

As you know, many monks or Tantra practitioners practice meditation and other spiritual activities after consuming hemps, cannabis, etc. I do not know how important or unnecessary this is. But I feel that without using intoxicants one can reach a higher position in spiritual development. One of the effects that these drugs have on the brain is the appearance of gaps between thoughts. By using this, the seeker starts getting deep into meditation. But these drugs have a lot of bad effects. So we should not use them. I have eaten cannabis eight to ten times just for fun and experiment. Half an hour after eating cannabis, I used to feel the effects of it. The body becomes lighter. The mind begins to open. In and Out of thoughts become clearly visible. The gap between thoughts also becomes apparent. All those sensations which we are not able to catch in the normal state of mind, we get able to catch them in the beginning after eating cannabis. We do 99% of our work spelled by habit. Our way of eating, the way of thinking, the way of taking bath, the way of washing, we go on doing everything habitually. You eat on time. You sleep on time. Our habit of fearing from the dark and the unknown. We keep doing everything habitually and we do not mind. We do not even realize that how badly we keep torturing ourselves every moment. We remain unaware of that there is an innocent consciousness within us that wants everything to be happened in an ideal way, everything to be done in a natural way. But we do not care for that at all. And every moment we keep suppressing that. People say, great atrocities are being done in the world. I say that we are torturing ourselves every moment. Our consciousness is purest of the pure. And we keep pouring all kinds of dirt on it. There are trillions of cells in our body. Also they want everything to be done naturally. We do not care for them at all. We lie, we get angry. Our consciousness suffers. We drink wine. Our cells suffer. We smoke. Our consciousness, our lungs, our mouth all undergo torturing. When we keep tobacco in our mouth, our mouth, nervous system and brain undergo torturing. Even if we have a habit of over-washing after toilet, our system has to undergo torturing. All this is known in the initial period after eating cannabis. Half an hour after eating cannabis, the body, mind and consciousness get opened. And they remain opened for about two hours. In that time we start catching all these things about how our body is reacting to our acts. How is our consciousness reacting? The feeling of sadness that occurs in the normal state is increased by hundreds of times at this time. Similarly, also the feeling of happiness increases hundreds of times. Rather the truth is that the feeling of happiness and sadness in our consciousness is actually hundreds of times greater. But we are not able to capture that feeling properly in the normal state. In the normal state, we are able to capture the feeling hundreds of times less only. Well, after eating cannabis, the mind becomes so calm that there is a long gap between each thought. By meditating at that time, one can enter into deep meditation. But after about two hours the situation starts changing. You have spent so much energy that you can no longer control your mind. Now your mind starts behaving as your enemy. The negative emotions accumulated inside you start to dominate you. And then gradually you fall into the grip of a hangover. That's why I believe that it is not right to consume cannabis for meditation, or other spiritual practices. It pulls you back instead of taking you forward. But if you practice meditation with burning desire with all your will, your body will automatically do whatever is needed to help you get deeper into meditation. Your brain starts producing such hormones, which completely calm your mind like cannabis or hemps do. Those hormones make you consciously intoxicated and they open your mind. But those hormones do not have any bad effect on you. If you have this kind of experience, a mild conscious intoxication without using a drug, then enjoy it to the fullest. You should drown yourself in this intoxication, so that you could surrender yourself in the lap of infinite.

Movements of parts of the subtle body

The subtle body is often experienced during meditation. You are in meditative state on mat or chair. And suddenly you feel that you are not sitting but your body. Where are you then? You find yourself standing behind that sitting body. You are sitting meditatively and suddenly you find that your body is moving. Your hands and feet are in motion. You find that you have two bodies, one sitting still and the other travelling. You are meditating and all of a sudden your astral body gets up and walks, passes through the walls or fly off the ceiling and as soon as you get worried, your astral body disappears in a moment and you return to the physical body. As you know; we are made of five bodies. In the normal state, we can feel only the physical body. But in the state of meditation we begin to become familiar with our other bodies as well. If you have such experience during meditation, then you should keep watching them with a witnessing attitude. These are the stairs, climbing which you enter the inner world.

Feeling emptiness throughout the body

You live in your body. That's why you think you are the body. The truth is that you live in this universe! Then why do not you feel that you are the universe? Just as you live in this universe, so you live in your body. You think of your body as "I". Think of your mind as "I". That's why there is a burden in the body and mind. The body remains heavy and full of your "I, me, my". While meditating, your relationship with "I" starts to weaken. So the body starts feeling lighter. The mind seems to be weightless. The body is already empty. When the earth is infinite times heavier than the body and the sun is infinitely heavier than the Earth and the universe is infinitely heavier than the sun, and they all move easily in the existence. Then how your body can be considered heavy! It's already light. Your "I, me, my" have made it to feel heavy and occupied. Your "I" is not you. Your "I" is a heap of your thoughts and deeds. You are your consciousness. Consciousness is omnipresent. You can take your consciousness out of your body and move it inside another body. You can take your consciousness to the sun, to the moon, to the stars. Your consciousness may be cosmic. Your consciousness can become bondless by being free from the "I". This is what happens while meditating. The "I" begins to disappear and the consciousness begins to open up and expand. So it seems that the body has become empty internally. The body is emptied of "I, me, my etc." It's a good experience. Witness it consciously. This is a sign that now your consciousness is spreading its wings to fly.

Body feeling weightless like hanging dry clothes

You must have read in the meditation guide book that 'feel the body weightless'. Feel like a dry hanging clothe. You can experience this in no time by doing this. Even if you do not try this, even after practicing meditation for a few days, you will start feeling like this. While meditating you will feel as if your body has become completely weightless like an inflated balloon. It has become so weightless that it can just fly. There is just a slight weight, which is stopping it from flying. You will also start feeling your body as hanging dry clothes. You'll feel like your entire spine has disappeared! You will feel whole middle part of your body like a vacuum. Hollow from inside like a bamboo. As if the body has moved out from clothe. Or like a hanging clothe. If you have such an experience, try to stay in this state for as long as possible. Or you just let this experience going on. Do not stop this.

And it is not that you will be able to experience this only when you are sitting in a posture and practicing meditation. You can have this experience anytime. When your energy is pure, your "I, Me, My" are weaken, you are deeply lost in love or devotion, or you get completely immersed in some work, even at that time you can have this experience. You start feeling weightless. That lyric must not have been written without experience, "Aajkal paawn zameen par nahi padte mere...(Nowadays my steps do not fall on the ground)..." You really feel like that. This happens because of inner purification, and inner rhythm. It's a good experience. This is a spiritual experience.

Experiencing divine vision – visualizing beyond the limits of the physical eye

This world is divine. But normally we do not see the divinity in this world. When you go deep into meditation, this world starts looking divine to you. Sometimes you are talking to your friend face to face. And suddenly while talking; it seems that physical distance between you and your friend has increased so much. Your friend looks far away from you. He begins to appear in a different aura. Shining like an effigy, like a statue. You feel that everything has gone too far from you and everything starts to look divine. Have you ever felt like this? Or you must have experienced such a thing while meditating, while doing some chanting or even while doing spiritual practices while sitting in front of your Guru or Guru's photo. All relative things seem either too big or too small. And the distance between you and the object seems increased.

To see the planets and constellations, you have to take the help of telescope. Earth can be seen from space. Or with the help of pictures sent from satellite, you can see the earth. But while meditating, you can see the whole universe with your eyes closed or open. While meditating, you can talk to your guru or someone who has reached deep into meditation. You can impress an ordinary person by sending thoughts while meditating. But do not get too bogged down in these things. The goal of meditation is not this but self-realization. But these experiences will definitely come your way. You have to pass through them without getting confused.

Experiencing the doorway to the unknown in middle of the forehead

When in the beginning you must have given suggestion to yourself that I am not the body. And then you must have tried to know yourself. So you must have been in a lot of trouble at that time. You are meditating. You are thinking that I am not the body. But you feel that you are the body. If your nose starts itching, then you feel that you are itching. If your leg hurts, then you feel that you are in pain. Gradually you are able to make a distance from the body. But then you become the mind. You become the thought. You wander from one thought to another. You become the emotion. You keep wandering between feelings. You think that I am not the mind. But you keep on feeling that you are the mind. Gradually, the hold of the mind weakens. Then you fall into the bondage of the chakras. You think that I am not the Third Eye Chakra. But you keep on feeling that you are the Third Eye Chakra. Your attention is centered in the center of your head. At that time you feel as if a cave has opened between your eyebrows towards outside. In the cave colored round waves are moving from inside to outside i.e. coming towards you, or going from outside to inside. If you are feeling like this, it means that your consciousness is rising from the body and mind and is being activated in your Third Eye Chakra.

It's a good experience. But do not stop here. You are not Chakra too. You have to awaken your Kundalini. You have to start with your Root Chakra. After passing through all the chakras, then one has to rise above the Third Eye chakra also. You cannot rise up into the sky without establishing your roots in the ground. Without strengthening or purifying your base, no matter how much you meditate on the Third Eye Chakra, you will not be able to fly. Even if you fly, you are sure to fall.

Experiencing some mystic activities little above the upper head

You must have seen the picture of yogis or monks absorbed in deep meditation. Their eyes are half closed and half open. You must have tried it as well. By doing this you will feel that your consciousness is getting integrated inside your head and it is trying to move inwards, in an oblique direction, towards the upper middle part of your head. After practicing this state for a few days, a path opens up. The energy of your consciousness passes through your forehead and enters middle of the head and emanates in the space from the upper middle part of your head. It means that your Sahastrara Chakra (Crown Chakra) gets awakened. You begin to feel that an energy field is moving horizontally at a moderate speed slightly above your head. You begin to feel a mysterious energy field above your head. You feel as if your skull has opened at upper side. You feel that your energy is freely going towards the sky and celestial energy is freely entering you. After doing this practice for some time, you start feeling your Sahastrara (Crown) Chakra active all the time. Or you are able to activate your Crown Chakra whenever you want. Then you start feeling that some activity is taking place between three inches below and three inches above your middle upper head.

Your Crown Chakra can be awakened even without conscious effort. In such a situation, you may not understand what is happening with you! You may be worried that your head is functioning abnormally! By being upset, you can even take yourself beyond the limits of insanity. That is why it is said that meditation, yoga (method of merging infinite within) etc. should be practiced only under the guidance of a qualified guru (spiritual teacher or guide). Meditation, Yoga, Chakras are all scientific disciplines. Just as wrong medicine can take your life, in the same way meditation and yoga done in the wrong way can also kill you. Or it can make you insane. Never mess with your Crown Chakra. This is the door between you and the subtle world. The subtle world is full of mysteries. Here we can find ourselves and we can also lose ourselves. If your mind is balanced, your thinking is scientific and your goal is self-realization; then only try to activate your Crown Chakra. If you want to attain miraculous powers, it is better that you keep yourself away from the Crown Chakra. Otherwise you will push yourself to dangerous and harmful situations.

Experiencing supernatural sounds and visuals

As you know, you cannot hear all the voices of existence. You cannot see many things as well. Your normal ears and eyes have limits. They have limited range. Your ears can hear within that range and your eyes can see within that range. But these limits do not apply to your consciousness. Even consciousness can enable your ears or eyes to hear or see beyond their limited range. Not only this, your consciousness can also hear or see without using your ears or eyes. It is the same with the rest of other senses. By practicing meditation, consciousness starts rising and awakening. Since the journey is new, so the consciousness itself moves forward in bewilderment. During that time the boundaries become hazy, intermingled with each other and are transcended. Since you are not yet fully awaken. Your consciousness is not free yet. It is tied to your mind, senses and thoughts. Therefore they and consciousness have effect on each other. Therefore, when the boundaries are transcended, the ears begin to hear the sounds outside the range, eyes and mind start seeing visuals outside the range.

And the truth is not just that. Many of visuals seen at that time and many of voices heard at that time are just your imagination. They are the creation of your mind. You undergo such experiences even when the memories of present and past lives stored in your mind and cells are released. When consciousness arises, all the events together produce multi effect. You may see terrifying creatures, which are in fact the fear of the unknown deep within you. You may see dancing fairies, which may be your imagination or dominated lust or your artistic heart. An old memory of your of this life or past life may emerge, which you are not aware of. But mainly these experiences happen because your consciousness is rising and you are transcending the boundaries. Do not get bogged down in whether the visuals and sounds you see are true or fiction or old memories. Just witness them. Let the visuals pass. Let the sounds pass. Do not be afraid of them. Do not allow yourself to flow in their temptation. Do not do anything with them. They will pass away. And you will be able to transcend the boundaries successfully. It is a good experience to hear sounds or see visuals while meditating. This is a sign that your consciousness is rising. You are going deep into meditation.

Receiving glimpses of past or future events

When you meditate, you begin to get calm down. When your consciousness starts connecting with the infinite, sometimes you start getting glimpses of past or future events. These events may be related to you or someone you know, or your close friends or even a country or society. It depends on what are you deeply attached to at that time or those days? For yourself or for someone else? You can see the events related to that. You can also try to know someone's past or future in deep meditation. If you are in doubt about your future, then you can see your future. If you do not like that future, then at the same time you can try to change that event with your will power and then you will see the changed event. At that time you are in a deep state of meditation. Whatever you think at that time, it is likely to come true in the future. But the thinking should be right and full of goodwill. In deep meditation, if the past or the future events are seen, it may be either simply because your consciousness is transcending the time. Or it could also be because existence is warning you. It is telling you that something needs to be done. If you start seeing the past or the future while meditating, then you will do what you should do. Since you are in deep peace at that time and your consciousness is connecting with the infinite, you are in witnessing state. So you know exactly what to do. And you will do that.

Experiencing the rotation of different Chakras

As you know there are seven chakras in our body- Mooladhara chakra (Root Chakra) in the lower part of the spine, Swadhisthana chakra (Sacral Chakra) on the spine between Root Chakra and navel, Manipura chakra (Solar Plexus Chakra) on the spine behind the navel, Anahata chakra (Heart Chakra) on the spine in the center of the heart, the Vishuddhi chakra (Throat Chakra) behind the throat, the Agya chakra (Third Eye Chakra) between the eyebrows and the Sahastrara chakra (Crown Chakra) a little above the head. But only he experienced these chakras deeply, who has entered deep meditation. When you start meditating, your chakras become more active. You start feeling them. You can feel them moving horizontally right to left, front to back. These chakras are the centers of your various energies. They control your physical and mental activities. Also your physical and mental activities have an effect on your chakras. By adopting bad food habits, consuming intoxicants, continued polluted thinking impure your chakras. On the other hand, good food habits and positive thinking purify and empower your chakras. The chakras get purified also by doing meditation, yoga and other spiritual practices. Purification of the chakra makes you healthier. Your thinking becomes positive. You start attracting the best things out of existence for you. The spiritual journey, the journey of liberation passes through these chakras. The primary goal of meditation or spiritual practices is to cross these chakras by penetrating them one by one through our consciousness.

Sometimes you can feel these chakras without doing meditation or spiritual practices. For example if some dangerous situation comes all of a sudden, you start feeling your Root Chakra and Sacral chakras. You start feeling the sensation in those body parts. If someone sends negative energy or hate energy towards you, then you start feeling Solar Plexus chakra. You start to feel a circular energy field stretching and rotating near your navel. If there is an excess of love, separation or devotion, then you start feeling your Heart chakra. You start feeling like something is pulling inwards over there. Your hand suddenly starts moving to your heart. That's why lovers keep expressing the condition of their heart. In a difficult situation or in a challenging situation or when you start feeling inferior in front of the other person, then the throat starts drying without thirst. This may be related to the Throat Chakra. When doing difficult balancing tasks or working very mindfully, you begin to feel the Third Eye Chakra. You start feeling the pulse on your forehead. When you start doing something very efficiently, when you start having amazing ideas, you start feeling your Crown Chakra. You feel as if your head is opened at upper end and you are communicating with the sky. As if you are spread all over.

It is natural to experience chakras while practicing meditation. You should focus on your chakras one by one. Start with your Root Chakra. For a few days, focus on the Root Chakra only. Then meditate on the Sacral Chakra. In this way try to reach the Crown Chakra. Do not rush into it at all. As your chakras are awakened, you will start to feel a lot of changes in yourself. In these chakras your memory accumulated from your births is stored. When these chakras are awakened, those memories are rapidly released.

At that time you have to take care of yourself. For example, if you have a great fear of this life or of the past life, then that fear will be released immediately and for many days that fear will surround you badly. You will not understand why this fear is troubling you so much. Similarly, the repressed sex within you may suddenly release and dominate you. You will think that I am trying to walk on the spiritual path and my mind is running more towards sex.

Therefore, the awakening of the chakras should be done very carefully. Meditation on Chakra should be done only under the guidance of a guru or expert. So that he or she could handle your energy and feelings when needed. Otherwise you may become insane.

Feeling the body split into two parts

Sometimes while meditating you can feel like this. You can feel your body as a combination of two bodies, the right side and the left side. You can also feel their different energies. If both your energies are a little imbalanced, you will feel as if one part is more alive than the other. In such a situation, you should try to balance your energy.

I think this is the experience of Ardhanarishvara (Half Male and Half Female forming one Body). Both Shiva and Shakti are present in every man and woman. The man is hidden in the woman and the woman is hidden in the man. In deep meditation, man and woman can be awakened within us and we can feel two halves in our body. Or if there is an energy imbalance, we can feel our body split in two parts.

The mind getting lost in thoughts and then sudden awakening

You must have felt this often. You sit to meditate. You have turned ON some meditation music or you are chanting some mantra. You are constantly thinking of being thoughtless. When you become aware of this chain of thoughts, you start trying to be thoughtless. But then again the thought chain starts running. Then again you think about becoming thoughtless. This kind of sequence goes on. And bit by bit you go on falling into unconsciousness. Even in that unconsciousness, somewhere there remains the consciousness of being thoughtless, of being conscious. And suddenly your consciousness wakes up with a spark. You are completely filled with consciousness. You find yourself thoughtless. You feel your consciousness at higher level. After some time the chain of thoughts start again. You start falling into unconsciousness again. Again suddenly your consciousness awakens. This time you find your consciousness at a higher level than before. You try to keep the mind focused and thoughtless, but the mind getting lost in thoughts again and again... and experiencing sudden awakenings and then deep meditation - just like when trying to fall asleep you do not know when you fall asleep... but while meditating you know when you wake up...

Have you ever experienced like this? I have experienced this many times. And I think others must have had similar experiences. This is definitely the quality of our inner understanding, which knows that one cannot become thoughtless by trying. So it entangles us badly in a tiring chain of thoughts. We fight with that and get tired. We begin to drown into deep sleep or unconsciousness. And at that very moment the inner understanding takes over the outer understanding. And we start feeling conscious.

Pushing the consciousness forward in Third Eye and upwards in the Crown Chakra

In those days, I had started playing a game. I asked the person in front of me to take two long breaths and then think any number in mind. Then immediately I began to push my Third Eye chakra inside to outside. At the same time I repeatedly sent mental thoughts to that person to think a particular number. Then I asked the person if he or she has thought that particular number? That person got surprised because he or she had actually thought the same number. Similarly, I used to push the upper part of my head from inside to upwards and send imagined visuals in form of mental waves to the selected person or the person in front of me. I imagined the visuals in mind and through mental waves sent them to that person's mind. Then I asked the person that if he or she had seen such a visual? That person got bewildered because in fact that person had seen the same visuals. Later on I stopped doing such experiments. But I continued pushing the Chakras. This is a kind of chakra exercise or chakra fitness. This will make your chakras stronger. Your relationship with your chakras will deepen. Your control over your chakras will increase. You can do this exercise anytime even before, after or during meditation too.

Shifting focus of consciousness to any part of the body

You can do this exercise while meditating or at anytime. By practicing this you start feeling that you are not this body. Along with that healing of your body and mind takes place. To take the consciousness to any part of the body, try to have an inner look at that part. You do not have to look at that body part with your physical eyes. Just try to focus your inner mind on that body part. Try to feel that part with your complete consciousness. Bring that part into focus. In no time you will start feeling the flow of energy in that part or organ. You will feel as if the energy has become more active in that part as compared to other organs. When you focus your inner vision on some body part or organ, then your consciousness and energy start flowing towards that part of body. Similarly, when you concentrate at some part of your mind, then your energy and consciousness start flowing towards that part. By focusing your inner look at external objects, persons, places, events etc., you can channelize your energy there. The same process is adopted in distant healing. By doing intense meditation, you can send your energy to thousands of places simultaneously.

Manifestation of the subtle universe

When you start practicing meditation on a regular basis, gradually you start feeling change in yourself. Your attitude towards life starts transforming. You start to believe that life is so much more than what you see. This world is just a small part of life. You begin to feel connected to that greater part about which you do not know anything. You start looking at the smallest things with a broader vision. You start feeling that even a piece of grass is as important as a human being! Yet you are bound to crush them, to cut them, to uproot them! You start feeling small and helpless! You do not understand why existence has made the life so helpless? You are bound to hurt each other, to kill someone, to be killed by someone. This is written in destiny of every life. You start looking for the nothing and the absolute nothing everywhere in the material world. Your mind starts running towards the invisible, unreachable and unknown. Not only the world, but also your "I, me, my" seem empty to you. You accept yourself as such a consciousness which is unknown to itself. A fire starts burning inside you.

Then gradually the subtle world begins to reveal itself upon you. It starts giving momentary glimpses of it. Sometimes by showing a hole in the sky, it invites you to come across it. And sometimes it makes you to experience for a moment your ever-connected mysterious and unknown relationship with the entire creation. You feel that forgotten connection for a moment. Sometimes it holds your hand and takes you to its mysterious unknown realms. Sometimes it enters your heart in form of celestial divine music. Sometimes it makes you joyous and sometimes it makes your eyes to offer pious drops of tears. If you practice meditation and you are experiencing such experiences, it is natural and good. Let it happen.

Experiencing infinite expansion of consciousness

When you are engrossed in meditation, you are fully conscious. You become conscious and begin to feel your consciousness, the center of which is mostly located in your Third Eye chakra. You start feeling your consciousness in the Crown Chakra, Heart Chakra and other chakras as well. You begin to feel the power of consciousness. You see that your consciousness is controlling your body, mind, intellect and is higher than them. Slowly the dimension of your consciousness starts expanding. You begin to feel yourself much wider and broader than your body. You start feeling your consciousness spreading in the whole house, in the whole locality, in the whole city too. By expanding your consciousness further, you can feel it pervading the whole world. Then there comes a time when you realize that your consciousness is omnipresent. Your consciousness is present in living and nonliving both. The journey of expansion of consciousness is long. It starts with your Third Eye chakra.

Experiencing being detached from the world despite being worldly

After practicing meditation for a long time, you come to this state, when you start living as a witness all the time. To be in a spirit of witness simply means that you have become detached from everything. You start feeling that even though you are in the situation, you are free from the situation. Like even though you are in the world, you feel that you are detached from the world. You are doing all the necessary works. But you are not attached to them. You see someone laughing inside you. You see someone crying in you. But you remain untouched by both of them. As soon as the witnessing spirit awakens, consciousness becomes a burning flame. In its light and heat, all negativity, all unconsciousness, all vices start to burn and dissolve. Whenever you meditate, you should try to be in the witnessing spirit. For the rest of the time also, while working, while falling asleep, in sleep, in dreams, you should remain in the witnessing spirit. Meditation is the practice to witness. Gradually you become meditative. Then does not matter that you are sitting or walking or doing any other job, you remain in a meditative state. Initially to connect self with meditation, meditation has to be done in the form of activities. But later meditation becomes a way of life that is happening continuously. Meditation becomes your nature.

Transforming tendency

While practicing meditation, you start to feel that your attitude is changing. The speed of this change may be more or less in different individuals. But the change does happen. Slowly the inclination of your mind starts changing. It does not mean that you were earlier interested in commerce and while meditating you became interested in arts. But the useless, meaningless or deviating tendencies in your life will slowly start changing. For example, if you are addicted to alcohol, then maybe after some time your interest in alcohol starts decreasing and one day you stop drinking alcohol. Maybe you have greed. So gradually greed will disappear in you. Maybe you have a fear of the unknown or you have lack of self-confidence, then these tendencies will start changing gradually. Your negative tendencies will gradually start transforming into positive ones. If you are feeling such changes within yourself then you should not worry. Whatever is happening must be allowed to happen.

Experiencing body, mind, intellect and consciousness separately

As you go deeper into meditation, you begin to feel your body, mind, intellect and consciousness separately. You begin to see the rhythm between them. As long as there is a rhythm between them, everything remains calm, like a flower in bloom, like celestial music. When this rhythm is broken or disturbed, there is disturbance and noise. You try again to create the rhythm and everything becomes rhythmic again. If you are able to feel these four separately then you know that your consciousness is driving your body, mind and intellect. Through consciousness you can steer your body, mind and intellect in the right direction. Through consciousness you can create a rhythm between them. You can aggregate them. If the body, mind, intellect and consciousness are in one direction, then the power increases in an amazing way. Then the miracle ceases to be a miracle but becomes an ordinary event. It is auspicious if you start feeling the body, mind, intellect and consciousness separately while meditating. You must allow this experience to deepen. One should try to delve deeper into this experience.

CHAPTER THREE

Experimental Meditation

Meditation is a process of spiritual growth. There is nothing that meditation cannot touch or change. Meditation takes you beyond both life and death. But it should start with small things. If there is lack of concentration during study, if the memory is weak, if there is lack of discipline, if mind wanders, if any ability has to be increased, in any such situation, the goal can be achieved by using 'Experimental Meditation'. And the interesting thing is that you can create your own method of 'Experimental Meditation'. There is no binding, no restriction. And there should be no bondage in the path of liberation. To make it easy for you to understand the 'Experimental Meditation', I am sharing with you some experiments I have done.

Transforming probable future events through meditation

Many times in life you know what is going to happen or may happen in the near future. Like, the increasing quarrels between husband and wife are taking them towards divorce. The deteriorating health condition of the cancer patient will worsen in the coming days. Or the loss going on in the business will increase further in the next quarter. The number of corona patients will increase further in next month. Things like this, where you can almost accurately predict what's going to happen in the near future. What if that future is bad? Or what if you do not want those events in the future? In such a situation, you can try to change the possible future with help of experimental meditation. But your wish should be practical and it should not harm anyone. Otherwise the power will not work or your condition will get worse.

The future can be changed by using meditation. But its base depends on good intention and true prayer. You have to meditate deeply again and again. Just as Arjuna focused his attention on the eye of the fish, the same way you have to concentrate on your goal, the future you want. The future you want should be like a burning desire in your existence. When you sit to meditate, try to see what is possible in the near future. When you see visuals of that future event, start sending your energy to it. Pray to God or to the Supreme Power to change these events as per your wish. And then overlap the desired future events on those unwanted future event. If possible, erase the unwanted events by applying black paint on the canvas. Then start seeing the desired future. Start drawing it on your mental canvas. Feel happy. Be filled with gratitude. Be thankful. Keep doing this. There will come a time in a few days when you will start to feel that your future has changed. Now things will go according to your wish. It will be what you want. Still, you should keep doing this experiment for some time.

Negative energy hinders meditation

If there are negative energies, ghosts, tantras, practitioners of dark energies etc around you or in your house, they will hinder your meditation. Your mind will be bogged down. You will not even sit to meditate and even if you sit, you will get up very soon. Through meditation, you come in contact with the superpower, due to which a field of very positive and divine energy starts forming around you. Negative energies feel uneasy when they come in contact with this divine energy. Their negativity starts to burn. They start to feel like burning. They do not want to let go their badness or evilness. They do not want to get reformed. They want to remain as they are. That's why when someone around them starts meditating, they get scared. They get very angry. Their power begins to fade. Therefore, they do not want to make a delay. They do not want to take risk. So they immediately get active. Anyhow they try to distract the person from meditation. They may try to scare you. They may try to draw you towards sin. They may try to harm you. They may try to confuse you. The experimental meditation can be used to deal with such situations. You can use experimental meditation to convert negative energy into positive energy or to remove evil forces.

In those days someone had sent a wandering spirit to my house. I used to practice meditation every night. That spirit felt uneasy because of my meditation. That spirit did not tolerate my meditation for more than 20-25 minutes. Then suddenly my sister's 4-year-old son woke up from sleep and started crying loudly. And that spirit screamed in my mind, "Stop meditating! Otherwise I shall torture the child more!" She used to gripe the child vigorously. I have to stop meditating so that the child would not suffer. This happened every night. After a few days before sitting for meditation I started protecting the child by sending healing. Now that soul was unable to touch the child. So she angrily threw the dishes on floor and tried to scare me. When this did not help her, she started trying to mislead me by taking the form of a beautiful woman. Even this did not make any difference. Then she created an atmosphere of discord among the family members. But I did not stop meditating. And after a few days she stopped protesting. And after some time her existence was not felt in the house. Either that soul had left the house or it had got salvation. On the contrary, positive forces encourage you to practice meditation. They support you.

So if you practice meditation, then you should take care of these things. Negative forces should be kept away and positive forces should be invited. You should pray to them.

To neutralize black magic

I knew that someone was sending black magic towards me again and again. This was disturbing and painful for me. But I was keeping my peace. Because I knew that any day I can neutralize this black magic by doing intense meditation for two-three hours. And in fact, I used to do intense meditation occasionally like this. That's why no black magic was effective on me for long. At that time I did not meditate regularly. I used to do meditation when I feel thirsty for meditation or when black magic troubles me a lot. Still, meditation always gave me strength and kept me safe. Later, when I started to do meditation regularly, that person stopped sending black magic at all.

Similarly, I used to neutralize black magic from others too by using meditation and healing. I failed sometimes in neutralizing the black magic. But I was successful also many times. Before trying to remove black magic from others, you should make sure that you have protected yourself and you have the ability to handle that black magic. Otherwise, that person may get cured and you may get caught in the clutches of that black magic or it may have a bad effect on you. Once an acquaintance told his problem that suddenly something unknown happened to him. For last two weeks he is not able to make physical relationship with his wife despite his will. To cure him, I sent meditation healing to him. I did not tell him that I was sending healing to him. After two days he told that he has regained his lost ability. But after that I myself started facing the same problem. I felt that his problem had not been fixed but it had changed its' place. It was my fault that I did not protect myself before dealing with that. Then I did meditation healing for myself and I got rid of this problem. So you can use meditation to neutralize black magic or tantra. But you have to be very careful in this or else you can harm yourself. The same precaution should be taken while giving healing to a sick person. Otherwise, the disease can be transferred to you.

Tantric demon figurine left the body during intense meditation

Once a well wisher applied a terrible tantra on me and fixed a tantric demon figurine in my body. (Those who trouble us are actually our well-wishers, because they force us to hone our talents.) So that demon figurine used to get alive inside my body and cause a lot of troubles. When I tried to suppress the figurine by meditation, it used to bite me from inside. It used to hurt me. It used to climb up my spine and hurt me. Once I was badly irritated and I was determined that no matter how much trouble it may give me today, but I will drive it away. I started meditating deeply. The figurine started giving me troubles and pain. But I tolerated all and continued meditating. Ultimately my energy in meditation became so integrated that it became difficult for the figurine to stay inside my body. It came outside my body with a jerk. It stood on my thigh for a while. It was about 4 inches tall. It was a living fat demon figurine. It jumped out of my body and ran away like a coward.

Understanding, breaking and rebuilding of thought chains

Thoughts are our mental habits, subtle habits. When meeting different people, thoughts chains of different patterns start forming. This pattern is fixed for different persons, different situations. Different thoughts go on while eating. Different thoughts go on before going to sleep. Whatever the situation arises, the chain of thoughts made for it, starts running. Apart from habit, our ego controls our thoughts. It continues to justify itself through chains of thoughts. Apart from this, our eating habits also have an effect on our thoughts. Vibrant thoughts come on eating light digestible food. Fatty meals produce sleepy, fainting thoughts. Exercise not only energizes the body but also produces energetic thoughts. Our body, mind, intellect, consciousness are all connected to each other. When one is strong, the others also get strong. When one becomes weak, the others also become weak. That is why the spiritual seeker is forced to work hard for the purification of the body and mind. Though, his goal is to elevate his consciousness. He knows that his body and mind will last for a limited period. But without making the body, mind and intellect healthy and pure, he will not be able to raise his consciousness. Therefore, knowing the soil, the spiritual seeker works hard for years to purify his body and mind.

Normally we do not understand the reasons behind our chain of thoughts. We are not able to see the habits, ego, food habits etc. hidden behind them. That's why we feel that we cannot control our thoughts. The mind is ours. Wisdom is ours. Yet we begin to feel ruled by our own thoughts because we cannot stop thoughts. We are not aware of the ways to control our chain of thoughts. While meditating, our consciousness rises. At that point we are able to see our thought chain. Slowly we start to understand when what kind of thought chain is going on. We begin to understand its pattern. We begin to understand the factors that control it. Then we do not try to stop the thought chain by force. Rather, we start looking at our thought chain with a witnessing attitude, without any emotion. When we witness a thought chain and end emotional attachment with it, that thought chain begins to weaken. And while weakening, that chain of thought comes fewer times and remains for shorter time. And gradually it stops taking birth. Similarly, we control our food and drink, due to which we get freedom from unwanted thought chains. As we go deeper into meditation, our ego starts to weaken. Because of this, the thought chains driven by the ego also start to weaken. And since the greatest controlling force of thought chains is our consciousness. So by meditating, our consciousness starts rising, which affects our thought chains. Practicing meditation regularly gives us the ability to understand, break and change our thought chains.

To heal self and others

Through meditation, we can heal ourselves and others. This healing can be done to cure any physical, mental or spiritual problem. Siddhas (enlightened seekers/saints) have said, "Everything is just emotion!" Healing is a feeling. The healer acts on a higher level of consciousness. Whatever feeling he creates, if it is benevolent, then it starts actualizing. At a higher level of consciousness, we connect with cosmic energy. At that time, the cosmic energy becomes active to fulfill the feeling we create. Health, wealth, happiness, success, anything can be created from that feeling. The condition is that you should have unconditional love for everyone. You should have deep faith in your heart for the divine power. To heal yourself or others, you have to enter deep into meditation. When your mind becomes thoughtless, pray to the divine power for fulfillment of what you want. And then remain in a loving state and watch your prayer come to fruition in your mind. And then the decision should be left in the hands of God.

Change in your thought process changes the behaviour of others

Many times we get worried about the thinking of the other person for us. Sometimes we remain unhappy for the whole life because the thinking of a person is not right for us. Many times we keep trying our whole life, still we are not able to change the thinking of that person for ourselves. Just think, has your attitude towards you changed? Has your attitude towards that person changed? If your attitude towards you has not changed and your thinking towards that person has not changed, then how the thinking of that person for you can change! As such you are thinking unconsciously, and that person is also thinking unconsciously. Your thinking is influencing his thinking and his thinking is affecting your thinking. To change his thinking you have to change your thinking. Unless you change your thinking, how will he be able to change his thinking towards you?

You can change your thinking through meditation. By going deep into meditation, you have to analyze your thinking towards that person. Negative factors have to be analyzed. Recognize and accept your mistakes. You have to forgive that person from your heart. Because you know he or she is not thinking consciously. As thinking arises automatically due to various reasons. Then you have to forgive yourself too. As soon as you forgive yourself and that person, you will see that your thinking about that person has changed. Your negativity towards him has subsided. But it is possible that after some time your thinking towards that person will again become the same as before. And when you would meet him face to face, you would get upset again in the same way. Let it happen. You continue this experiment again and again by going deep into meditation. Again and again forgive yourself and that person. Not only this, shower a lot of unconditional love on yourself and on that person again and again. Gradually you will see that your thinking has become neutral for that person. And when you come face-to-face with that person, then you will see that also his or her thinking has become neutral for you.

To purify body, mind, thoughts etc.

Divine power awakens within you by doing meditation. Presence of light removes darkness, but the presence of divine energy transforms negative energies. That is purification. This purification takes place at all levels; body, mind, thoughts, conscience etc. So for purification you have to do regular meditation. One thing has to be remembered here that if you meditate for 1 hour a day, then in that 1 hour the divine power works on you. But for the remaining 23 hours, negative forces keep working on you. Even negative forces do not want to be transformed. That's why they work on you for 23 hours so that you could quit meditation. They struggle for their existence so that even if you keep practicing meditation, they could survive. So you have to be aware during the remaining 23 hours too. Only then purification will take place. Otherwise, it will be like a game to purify and to get impure for your whole life. It is like go one step forward and again one step backward.

By the way, meditation alone is enough for purification. The work of the energy of meditation is to do the purification. But for faster purification, you can pray for purification before, during and after meditation. You can try to watch in your mind your negativity being burnt into ashes. By doing this the speed and power of purification increases.

Connecting with nature and feeling oneness with creatures

In this infinite existence, everyone and everything, not only humans but also animals, birds, plants, is absolutely alone. On the basis of our convenience and geographical reasons, we form small and big groups and name them family, society, country etc. We get the illusion that we are not alone and our group is with us. Those who do not have anyone to share their emotion, many times they form a deep emotional relationship with street dogs. Those whose family is very big, they form small groups in their own family. Earlier there were tribes who used to fight amongst themselves. Then small villages were formed. Then small states were formed. Now small countries have taken form. People of a country think that they are one. The people of other countries are not their own. Countries are ready to fight with each other. Earlier clans fought in the same way as nations fight today. After a few hundred years, when civilizations outside the earth would invade the earth, the people of the whole Earth will become one. Every resident of the Earth will unite and will fight against the aliens. Then every person on the earth will feel oneness for each other. Then Indians and Chinese will not consider each other outsider or unfamiliar. Just like today North Indians and South Indians consider each other one family. But the truth is that everyone is absolutely alone in this infinite existence.

But the truth is also that the whole existence is intertwined. Our body was once a part of the earth. Once this earth was part of the sun. Once this sun was part of the universe. This universe was once a part of Mahashunya (absolute zero). Our body will be part of the earth again in the future. In the same way the earth, the sun and the universe will all merge back into the absolute zero. In this way, all are one. Apart from this, there is an unbreakable relationship between everyone. Like the sun is connected to us by heat, light rays. It is pulling us continuously with a force. The moon has its' effect on every drop of water on the earth. Invisible waves are having an effect on everything. The exhaled breath of one organism is entering into another organism. Some part of its life energy also remains in that exhaled breath. Life force is getting mixed up like this. In this way, we are connected with the entire nature. But because of the hard cover of our "I, Me, My" we feel that we are separate and nature is separate.

With continuous practice of meditation, the cover of "I, Me, My" starts melting, it becomes sparsed. We begin to feel the relationship between nature and ourselves. We begin to understand the continuous dialogue between self and nature. How we think, how we behave, it all has an effect on nature. Accordingly, also nature returns to us through things and creatures including human. You can see that some people are surrounded by ocean of love. Thousands of millions of loving people are present around him or her. Surely he or she must be giving love to nature. And nature is returning the same love through people. And when nature returns, it returns in manifold because the capacity of nature is very high. Nature does not lack anything. From worst to best, it has everything more than enough. When we feel oneness with nature, we fall in love with trees, plants, animals and birds, pebbles and stones. Seeing the bondage of sorrow, suffering, pain, ignorance, attachment and illusion prevailing in the world, the same love gets transformed into compassion. With this feeling, the yogis must have said, "Have mercy on the living beings." You too will have the same feeling. You will become loving, for yourself and for nature. You can use meditation to reach this level of consciousness.

CHAPTER FOUR

Benefits of practicing meditation

Meditation is beyond loss and benefit. Meditation is the way to liberation. Loss and gain lose their existence on the path of liberation. But not everyone wants liberation. Rather, it would be correct to say that only a few of them need liberation. Some want money, some want health, some want extraordinary strength. If the desires are sincere, good, practical, then meditation can make them come to fruition. Meditation is always beneficial. Practicing meditation regularly has innumerable benefits. Some of those benefits are:-

Improved skills

Regular practice of meditation increases the concentration of the mind. Intelligence develops. Physical abilities increase. Illusions disappear. One gets free from depression. One feels excitement, enthusiasm and joyfulness. The fear of success-failure, defeat-victory ends. The doer disappears. Discipline comes in life. Goals become clear. Your own energies start working in totality. So whatever we do, we do in a better way. That is why meditation should be practiced regularly in school. Meditation should be made an essential part of education. This will lead to the full development of the abilities of the children and the standard of humanity will improve.

Self-realization and unfolding the true nature

We have been told since childhood – the body is mortal. The soul is indestructible, immortal, beginningless and infinite. Gradually this philosophy enters our belief system. We begin to believe that we are souls. We are Eternal, Infinite, Fireproof, Immortal etc. But we do not know ourselves. We have not experienced self-realization. We only know our body and mind. But we are made to believe that we are soul. We have unknowingly accepted something which is a big lie about ourselves; so it has become normal for us to be a liar. Wearing masks, 'being something - pretending something else', is it not really a small thing for us? To cheat, to deceive, to misguide, to lie have they not become part of our personality more or less? We think we are deceiving others. But first we deceive ourselves. We are the body from head to toe. But we talk about the soul. We do not know our soul. But reading and listening make us to think that we know God. Same is the case with all religions. That is why human beings are becoming hollow all over the world. Body and mind have taken the form of soul. And we have imprisoned God in the boundaries of temples and mosques. How to get salvation? We have to rise above our body and mind and find our soul. Unless the soul is found, God will not be found either.

By practicing meditation regularly, we learn to transcend our body and mind. We begin to get glimpse that we are something other than our body and mind. Our soul begins to manifest. We get to know our true nature. But care has to be taken that we do not start deceiving ourselves even in meditation. We have to stop playing with our borrowed knowledge. Everything else has to be disbelieved except the awakened consciousness. We have to feel the pain of ignorance. Name, form, caste, sect, knowledge, we have to start our journey by taking off all these shells. We have to create a blaze in our chest to find ourselves. We have to burn in the fire of meditation. Slowly we will start to understand ourselves. We will begin to realize our true nature. Then we will learn to wear name, form, caste, sect as temporary masks. We will begin to feel our existence, which is free from name, form, caste, and creed and which is comprehensive.

Deciding life goals

Children are asked in school – what will you become? Some says that he or she will become a doctor. Everyone takes the name of a different profession. If you look carefully you will find that their main goal is livelihood. And their choice is less heart oriented but more mind oriented. They know that doctors earn more and their profession is respectful. This is the wish of their parents. It is not that the child has a strong desire to service the sick. Even if he talks about service, the elders must have put this in his or her mind. Becoming a doctor cannot be the goal of life. It is just a livelihood. The goal of life is the full development of one's abilities. The goal of life is to blossom completely. To achieve that goal, one should choose a career of his or her choice. Livelihood should not be given more importance than earning bread and butter.

Otherwise we will be stuck to it. And that livelihood will be taken away from us at the time of retirement. And we will be zero. And then we will neither have that energy nor the time to fix our goals. Under compulsion, we start carrying our past. Army man starts living as ex-army man. Worker starts living as ex-worker. This is a sad incident with humanity. Humanity is being destroyed just for the sake of livelihood. Today there are more than 130 crore people in India. Few corrupt leaders are spoiling the system. And 130 crore people are unable to do anything. Why? Because 130 crore people are spending their whole life behind livelihood. At the age of three years, the child is sent to school, so that the child could earn bread after twenty years. And after that the child continues to earn bread for the rest of his life. He earns bread and talks about corruption. And if some of them come into politics, it is to earn bread only. God created the world based on life. We have made that world based on money. Earning money has become the biggest goal of the whole world. Even most of the babas, sadhus (saints, monks) etc. are doing the business of Babagiri (befooling devotees by pretending a saint or monk) only for money. How ridiculous this situation is, it can be understood from the fact that from beggar to billionaire, trillionaire, everyone is constantly engaged in earning money. If a poor thinks to earn money then it is understandable. But the life goal of the trillionaires is also the same - to earn money. If someday human civilization touches the zenith then I believe that at that time there will be no such thing as money in the world.

By practicing meditation regularly, gradually our real goal becomes clear. Then we earn money to live. We do not live to earn money. Then we do our best for the betterment of our society. We can serve the patients by becoming doctors. We can protect the borders by becoming soldiers. Simultaneously we put efforts towards our real goal. We do not wander. Our goal is self realization. And such a person keeps on moving towards his goal while protecting himself from lust, anger, attachment, greed, ego etc. That person fulfils his social responsibilities. And whatever he does, he does with honesty and hard work. He does it successfully.

To know, accept and improve own shortcomings

Meditation practitioner knows his shortcomings very well and very much accepts it. Sometimes we feel that we know our shortcomings. But it may not be true. Suppose Rahul gets angry very quickly and sees it as his shortcoming. But he does not know the reason behind his anger. Because he is given less love, so he gets angry very quickly. So Rahul's real shortcoming is getting less love. Until he fulfils this lack of love, he will not get rid of anger.

There are many shortcomings in every human being. His biggest drawback is that he does not know himself. After that there are flaws in his personality. There are shortcomings in his health, in his abilities. While practicing meditation, we start seeing all our shortcomings. In meditation one focuses one's mind in his inner life rather on external world. So, inward awareness increases which leads to discovery of one's shortcomings. We see that our consciousness is imprisoned within the body and mind. We start seeing different kinds of shortcomings within us, which others do not see. We see how our mind is clogged with happiness and sorrow, honor and disgrace. We see that existence is infinite, in which we are tiny parts physically. We see that even a small virus has the power to threaten the very existence of the great human race. We see how negligible our presence in infinite existence is, yet we have the capacity to hold this universe. We see that we are so insignificant as well as we do have potential to become great.

Then we start focusing more on our real shortcomings. We also try to remove the shortcomings of worldliness, not for prestige, but for a better individual character. In order to live in a practical way in the world, we remove the shortcomings which are necessary to overcome. But we put all our strength into removing our real shortcomings. Thus we can become complete human beings and we can attain the self. We can free ourselves and show others the way of liberation.

For multidimensional development of consciousness

With regular meditation our consciousness achieves multidimensional development. A person ignorant of meditation remains ignorant of his consciousness. One who is aware of his own consciousness, he has the experience of meditation. Even if he has never heard the name of meditation. While immersed in meditation, he can write poetry, sculpt a statue or draw a picture. He can provide food to the hungry. He does all this with the inspiration of consciousness only. But with regular practice of meditation, the development of consciousness is possible. We have heard that consciousness is omnipresent. But we have no experience of this. By practicing meditation we can experience the omnipresence of consciousness.

As our consciousness grows, so do our abilities. We begin to become proficient in arts-skills. We begin to own a multidimensional personality. Gradually our consciousness starts getting higher. We start feeling free from the limitations of time and space. We become able to awaken the consciousness of others with our consciousness. Our consciousness becomes capable of going anywhere, anytime. There comes a time when we see that our consciousness and the consciousness of others are not separate. Consciousness is one. Our circumscribed individuality melts into the ocean of universal consciousness. We merge into infinity. We become infinite. The drop becomes the ocean.

Afterword

Thank you for reading "Meditative Moments of a Seeker". I wish you to go deeper and deeper into the moments of meditation. I request you to share your thoughts, experiences and your review of this book with me and readers.

My books are available on Amazon, Smashwords, Kobo, Apple Books, Google Play Books, Barnesandnoble, Scribd, Flipkart, Notionpress and other stores. A few links given below:

https://www.amazon.in/dp/B09VPRZHFN

https://www.amazon.in/-/hi/ANURAG-PANDEY/e/B083STJ8F8

https://play.google.com/store/books/author?id=ANURAG+S+PANDEY

https://notionpress.com/author/397403

https://www.kobo.com/us/en/ebook/meditative-moments

https://www.flipkart.com/good-evil-supernatural/p/itm49982a430f1dc

https://books.apple.com/au/author/anurag-pandey/id818684991

https://www.barnesandnoble.com/s/anurag%20pandey

https://www.smashwords.com/profile/view/ANURAGPANDEY

Or Google Anurag S Pandey. You can send me your valuable suggestions through email. You can also connect with me on Twitter and Facebook.

anuragspandey@gmail.com

https://twitter.com/ANURAGP64628371

https://www.facebook.com/anurag.pandey.98031
https://www.facebook.com/HalfCookedThoughts
Anurag S Pandey
Bhubaneswar, India

Printed by Libri Plureos GmbH in Hamburg, Germany